How to Invest in Real Estate with Little or No Money Down

Other McGraw-Hill Books by Robert Irwin

How to Invest in Real Estate with Little or No Money Down

Robert Irwin

McGraw-Hill

New York   Chicago   San Francisco   Lisbon   London
Madrid   Mexico City   Milan   New Delhi   San Juan
Seoul   Singapore   Sydney   Toronto

Library of Congress Cataloging-in-Publication Data

Irwin, Robert.
　　How to invest in real estate with little or no money down / by Robert Irwin.
　　　　p.　　cm.
　　Includes index.
　　ISBN 0-07-143999-4 (alk. paper)
　　1. Real estate investment—United States.　　2. Real estate investment—United States—Finance.　　3. Real estate management—United States.
　I. Title.

HD255.I7813 2005
332.63'24'0973—dc22

2004008158

Contents

How to Invest in Real Estate with Little or No Money Down

1

Acquiring Real Estate Wealth

I don't like "get rich quick" books. I don't believe in them any more than I do in the Tooth Fairy. Very few people I've known got rich quick; and of the few who did, only one hung onto her money for any length of time. Of the few cases I've seen, the story is typically rags to quick riches and just as quickly back to rags.

On the other hand, I've known a great many people who have gotten rich over time . . . and kept their wealth. They accomplished this feat by steadily working at it. They had successes and a few failures, but over the years their net worth grew and grew until it was in the millions. For some it took 10 years, others 20, still others an unusually quick 5 years and, for a few, an entire lifetime.

Most began very humbly with very little. Some were immigrants. Most were young when they started, but many were middle aged and late entries.

Those who made it came from all kinds of professions—two butchers, a produce clerk, a couple of accountants, several carpenters, quite a few white-collar workers, and even more blue-collar workers.

Some were men; many were women. Almost all had other full-time lives: raising a family, working at a career, tending to a business, traveling. All worked at it part time. There was little they had in common—except for one thing. They all invested in real estate. (This is not to say that you can't make money elsewhere—you can. But that's a different book.) Of course, this is not to say that those who got wealthy in real estate avoided other investments. They didn't. They owned the usual—stocks and bonds. Many owned more esoteric investments such as gold, silver, and even stamps and rare coins and paintings. But over time, where they made their real money, where their wealth came from, was real estate.

I remember once talking with a successful magazine publisher. He had three titles all distributed nationally on newsstands. (I'm sure you would recognize some of them if I mentioned their names, but he's a good friend and I agreed to keep his story anonymous in exchange for using this anecdote.) We were talking about wealth, and I pointed out that he had done very well for himself. He had a small publishing empire.

"Yes," he replied. "But the only real money I've ever made was in real estate."

I was shocked, until he explained. It turned out that over the years, he had plowed his profits from the magazine company into property, industrial and commercial buildings. Some years the magazines made good money; other years they lost. Overall, they provided him with a handsome income. But the real estate he had purchased had steadily grown in value to the point where it had made him very wealthy.

I know another fellow, Larry, a produce clerk in a grocery store. I don't believe he ever made more than $12 an hour. (He retired several years ago.) But he bought real estate on the side. (I know, because I sold him a lot of it!) He bought single-family homes, duplexes (two rental units together) and fourplexes (four units together). He seldom had much cash on hand. He retired modestly in a small house when he was in his fifties. But his net worth (measured by how much he had in equity in properties) was in the many millions. And he could realize it (get at the money) when he wanted to by refinancing or selling one of his properties.

A woman I know, Sylvia, ran a beauty parlor in Las Vegas. She saved all her tips in a jar and used them to buy a small house. Then another. Then another. And soon she had over a dozen rental homes, and her rental income after expenses (positive cash flow) eventually far exceeded her beauty shop income.

The point of these examples is that it doesn't make much difference who you are, what you do, where you come from, how you invest your other money, or how much cash you have. The only thing that counts is that at least part of the time you invest in real estate. Over the years, no matter what happens elsewhere, your real estate investments should lead you to wealth.

"The Only Investment That Always Goes Up . . . Not!"

Broadcasters, reporters, and investment advisers for stock and bond companies had a field day with the above quote back in 1992. It was the early 1990s, and the real estate bubble of the late 1980s had popped. Prices were no longer going up; some were falling; and some people who bought homes at the top (particularly those who bought with loans bigger than the home's value) suddenly discovered that they owed more than their homes were worth. They were "upside-down" and were sometimes heard to remark, "But, I always thought real estate only went up in value!"

TRAP

When you're "upside-down" you owe more than your home is worth.

The reporters said that the great real estate recession of the 1990s proved beyond a shadow of a doubt that property prices went down as well as up. It proved that real estate was just as volatile an investment as stocks, bonds, or anything else.

But was it?

Some areas of the country such as Riverside County in California and parts of Los Angeles, as well as parts of Massachusetts and the Northeast, saw prices drop as much as 25 to 30 percent. A home that had been worth $200,000 was suddenly worth only $150,000 . . . or less.

Worst of all, in those areas there were no buyers. Real estate in the best of markets is an illiquid investment—it's hard to sell and cash out. When the market is really bad, it's all but impossible.

Yet there were some out there who weren't pulling their hair out lamenting the hard times and how real estate goes down as well as up. Instead, they were gobbling up properties, as quickly, as cheaply, and in as much quantity as they could. They weren't concerned that prices were slowing or dropping. As soon as they saw they could break even on renting out a home, they scooped it up. They could care less about the doomsayers. All they wanted to do was to accumulate as much property as possible—to buy and hold, waiting for the big turnaround. They believed that real estate always went up, eventually.

Well, of course that turnaround came. Did it ever! In recent years prices for real estate in most areas have almost doubled. In some areas they've actually tripled!

But what about those who bottom-fished during the recession of the early 1990s? They made out like bandits; they had huge profits.

How did they know the market was eventually going to go up? Were they clairvoyant? Did they have special knowledge?

I doubt they were psychic enough to see the future, but I suspect they probably did have special knowledge. And that special knowledge probably came from the Department of Housing and Urban Development (HUD) and was available to anyone who cared to look. It showed that the *average prices* (add all the prices and divide by the number of homes) for single-family homes across the United States as well as the *median price* (as many are priced above as below) for homes across the United States going back about 40 years never went down. The prices, both median and average, *across the United States* only went up! (It might not always have been up by much, in some bad years only a few hundred dollars, but the trend was always upward.)

Don't take my word for it. Check it out for yourself. Go to the Department of Housing and Urban Development's Web site and look into the information on their periodical charts. (As of this writing, the Web site is *www.huduser.org/periodicals/USHMC.*)

Yes, prices in different areas of the country did drop, sometimes precipitously, particularly in the Northeast and some other areas. But overall across the country, prices continued to rise, enough to even those drops out. And this was during the worst real estate recession in modern times.

The point here is not that real estate prices don't go down. They certainly do and may do so in your area. But overall and over time, certainly over the past 40 years and actually going back as far the founding of this country, real estate prices have always *trended* upward. The reason, as Will Rogers used to quip, is simple, "They aren't making any more of it!"

TIP

There's a moral here. Real estate is a great investment to be in. And when times turn bleak and everyone else is selling, it's an even better time to be in!

Of course, I'm assuming that as you read this, the market hasn't collapsed. (If it has, stop reading, get out there, and buy!) For you, the market's either strong or at least stable. If I've made my case, even in strong markets you should by now be eager to get out there and make some real estate profits. But how exactly do you do it, particularly if you have little to no cash?

How Money Is Really Made in Real Estate

The operative word is *leverage*. While most people have heard that real estate offers enormous financial leverage, few really understand how it works. You're going to be one of the knowledgeable few.

Leverage basically means that you buy property with other people's money. You put in little of your own. Indeed, a basic tenet of real estate investing is that the less of your money you can put into the deal, the greater your chances for profit (and, as we'll shortly see, for loss as well).

Perhaps you've seen this sort of thing in operation with stocks. You want to buy a hot stock that you think will soon go up in price. It costs $20 a share and you have $2000 to invest. That means that you can buy 100 shares. It's quite easy to see that if you buy 100 shares at $20 and the stock goes to $40 a share, you've doubled your money to $4000.

However, what if you could buy twice as many shares for the same $2000?

You may very well be able to do just that by buying on margin. Here you might put down only 50 percent of the price of the stock and, for a fee, a brokerage company might put up the other 50 percent. In other words, you've leveraged half the value of the stock. You only put up $10 for each $20 share of stock you bought. With your $2000 you now control 200 shares instead of 100 shares.

Now if the stock goes up to $40 a share, you've quadrupled your money. Because you have twice as many shares, your original $2000 jumps to $8000. Further, to double your money, the stock no longer has to double. With only a 50 percent increase in share price, you can double your investment; it only has to go up by half. You get much more bang for the buck because you control twice as many shares with the same investment cash. That's called *leveraging* your investment, and savvy stock investors do it all the time.

Of course, stocks are far more volatile than real estate. And there is always the chance that your stock might go down as well as go up. With a 50 percent leverage position, when the stock goes down you'd lose money twice as fast as you would by buying the stock outright at 100 percent a share. If the stock fell to $10 a share, all of your money would be lost. That's the risk with stocks.

Real estate leveraging works in a similar way, only a whole lot better. One of the big differences between the stock market and real estate is volatility. Stocks are highly volatile. Real estate is relatively low in volatility. While stock and bond prices bounce up and down on a daily basis, real estate prices move glacially. If real estate prices go up by 10 percent in a single year, it's considered an enormous increase. (Of course, in recent years we've seen some spectacular increases in value on the order of 25 percent per year, but that's hardly sustainable.) Most investors in real estate are very happy if prices just go up by 5 percent a year on average.

Further, as we've already seen during the dot.com crash of the early 1990s, while the entire stock market can drop in value by 50 percent or more in just two or three years, real estate overall tends not to go down in value, overall. Yes, some regional markets may drop, but at the same time other regional markets may be going up. In real estate overall what tends to happen is that the rate of increase slows but only rarely turns negative.

This has important ramifications for investors. One of the biggest is that because real estate is so stable an investment over time, individuals and institutions are willing to offer very high *loan-to-value* (LTV) financing.

TIP

Remember LTV (loan-to-value). It's a key to getting little or no cash financing.

Going back 50 years, it was common for lenders to offer 80 percent LTV. That means that for every two dollars you put into the property, the lender would put in eight dollars. You could leverage 80 percent.

Currently, times are much better. If you're an investor, some lenders will offer 90 percent LTV. For every *one* dollar you put into the property, lenders will offer *nine* dollars. You're leveraging 90 percent.

In later chapters we'll see how to buy property with lenders putting in 19 dollars for every dollar you put in. In some cases, they'll put in the entire amount, which allows you to purchase with 100 percent LTV or zero-down financing—no cash down payment. You're leveraging 100 percent!

Before you turn to those chapters, however, let's see how this high leveraging affects your investment returns. We'll assume that you buy a property for 5 percent down. (Remember, later on we'll see how to purchase for less, but for now let's take a middle-of-the-road leverage scenario.)

We'll assume that the property costs $300,000. Your LTV is 95 percent, so you'll need to put down 5 percent or $15,000.

Now let's say the property goes up 5 percent in value the first year you own it. What's your *paper* profit?

If you said 5 percent, you weren't thinking of our stock example. The way savvy investors figure their real estate profits is not on the value of the property, but on the value of their cash investment. If you put in $15,000 and the property goes up by $15,000 (5 percent of the property's full value in our example) the first year, you've doubled your money. It's called *cash-on-cash investing*.

Still don't see it? Think of it this way: Your original loan amount was $285,000 on a $300,000 investment. You put $15,000 down.

The property went up $15,000 to a total value of $315,000. Just subtract the amount you owe on the loan ($285,000) from the value and you get $30,000. That's twice the cash you put in. On paper, at least, your investment has doubled.

Okay, you may be saying. You've just proved that real estate can be as good as the stock market. You can double your money in both.

Actually, we've done much more. Remember, in order to double your money in stocks, the stock has to double in price. Even buying on the margin, it has to go up by 50 percent in value.

In our real estate example, the property only has to go up 5 percent in value (assuming you only put 5 percent down) to double your money.

TIP

 Real estate values for single-family homes in the United States for the past 30 years have increased in value *an average* of 6.5 percent per year. (Of course, there's no guarantee this rate or trend will continue.) (*Source:* HUD.)

Further, in real estate the chances are that the property may continue to increase, on average, by around 5 percent or more each year. That means that some years it might go up by 7 or 8 percent and other years by only 2 or 3 percent. You might get really lucky and get a 10 percent or more year or two and really unlucky and get a 1 percent or less (even into negative numbers) year or two. But on average, over the long haul, chances are you might hope to get around 5 percent a year—or better.

This means that the original money you invested continues to multiply as long as you own the property.

10-Year Growth of Original $15,000 in Home Purchased for $300,000 That Appreciates 5 Percent Per Year

Year	Value Increase of Prop.	Value Increase of Investment
1	$315,000	$15,000
2	330,750	30,750
3	347,251	47,251
4	364,613	64,631
5	382,844	83,844

(Continued)

Year	Value Increase of Prop.	Value Increase of Investment
6	401,986	101,986
7	422,085	122,085
8	443,190	143,190
9	465,349	165,349
10	488,617	188,617

After 10 years your original $15,000 investment is now worth $188,617 on paper. By comparison, if you had stuck the same $15,000 in the bank to collect interest at 5 percent, it would be worth $24,433. Remember, in our example you're in effect getting the benefit of 5 percent compounded on a $300,000 property, even though you've only invested $15,000. Your original money doubles and more every year. That's the power of leveraging.

In addition, during those years of ownership, you are also paying down the mortgage. At the end of 10 years your equity buildup as a result of mortgage payback is $46,455. (At the end of 20 years it would $141,075.) Add that roughly $46,000 of 10-year payback to the $188,617 from the above chart and suddenly your profit on paper is $235,072. On an original $15,000 investment!

Further, unlike with stocks, you don't have to be continually looking for new hot issues to purchase. After all, how often do you really find a stock that goes up 50 or 100 percent in value? And in order to find that really hot one, how many losers do you end up buying?

Also, unlike stocks, you're not likely to have those long drought periods when prices drop by half or more.

TIP

When was the last time you heard of any piece of property falling in value by 50 percent or, as has happened to many, many stocks, by almost 100 percent?

And that's how money is made in real estate. Let's be sure we've got the picture. It's a two-step process.

How Money Is Made in Real Estate

Step One: Highly leverage your investment.

Step Two: Let it sit and make you money.

A Part-Time Career

Step Two is the reason that so many real estate investors do it part-time. It's simply not a business that requires your full-time efforts. You buy a property using leverage. You rent it out. And you let it pay for itself while boosting your profits. If you let it sit, over time you'll find it will make you wealthy.

Before experienced investors begin tearing out pages, let me add that there will be occasions, sometimes very trying occasions, when you'll need to focus on the property and devote all your energies to it. This can happen when a tenant doesn't pay rent, or when there are maintenance or repair issues. However, if you buy wisely (buy a good property) and rent wisely (rent to a good tenant), these hard times should be at a minimum. (Check into Chapter 10 to see how to do this.)

All of which is to say that real estate affords investors the opportunity to continue their regular careers and their normal lifestyles while they invest. That's one reason that so many blue-collar as well as white-collar workers own property. That's why retail clerks and accountants, welders and entrepreneurs, immigrants and seventh-generation families all invest in real estate. It's the American road to wealth. For a vast majority of people, it's the *only* road to wealth.

The Other Reality of Real Estate Investing

Thus far we've talked as if finding and buying investment property and watching your profits roll in were as easy as rolling off a log.

It's not.

If it were, the country would be filled with nothing but millionaires. (As it is, millionaires are only about 1 percent of the population, which is still probably higher than any other country on earth, with the possible exception of the oil-rich lands of the Middle East.)

There are at least two difficulties that you must overcome in order to be a successful real estate investor. Both are surmountable. But, it's here where shrewd investing (the kind you learn, in part, from a book like this) pays off.

They are *negative cash flow* and *transaction costs*. We'll deal with them extensively in later chapters, but for now, here are the problems they present.

Negative Cash Flow

We've talked about buying with little or no cash down. Indeed, getting into real estate on that basis is the basic theme of this book. However, the less money you put into a property, the more difficult it becomes to break even.

Part of the reason is that in addition to a mortgage payment, as a landlord you'll also be paying property taxes and insurance. And occasionally there will be rent-up costs as well as periodic maintenance, repairs, and vacancies.

Add up all of these on a monthly basis and you get what many in real estate like to call your "nut." Like a squirrel, this is the amount you need to bring in each month to survive, to break even on the property.

Monthly "Nut" on a Rental Property

- Mortgage payment
- Taxes $(1/12^{th})$
- Insurance $(1/12^{th})$
- Rent-up costs (averaged over 5 years)
- Maintenance (averaged over a year)
- Repairs (averaged over 10 years)
- Vacancies (averaged over a year)

Of course, the single biggest element usually remains the mortgage payment, which gets bigger the less cash you put into the property. Add the mortgage payment to the others, and it can quickly add up to a substantial sum. Altogether this is what it will cost you each month to operate the property. If you make more, you'll be able to put cash into your pocket (a "cash cow"). If you make less, you'll need to take cash out of your pocket (an "alligator"—it bites you each month).

You Don't Want an Alligator

I don't have an alligator as a pet, and I hope you don't either. The reason is that they have nasty big tails and even nastier and bigger appetites. And they have this very nasty habit of biting whatever looks like food, meaning you and me.

Most good rentals bring in cash each month, or at the least break even. But you can have a bad rental and, if you do, it's like an alligator. When your monthly cash expenses exceed your monthly cash income, you're in a negative cash flow position. That means that each month you need to take money out of your wallet to meet your expenses. You've got an alligator biting your behind. Too often the less cash you put in, the bigger the alligator you end up with.

TIP

Part of the negative cash flow may be met by taking depreciation on your property. This may or may not be available to you as an annual write-off against income depending on your financial situation. See Chapter 12.

The bigger the hemorrhage from your wallet, the bigger the alligator. The problem for those putting little to no cash down quickly becomes "How much negative cash flow can you handle?" How big an alligator can you have biting you each month?

For some people, putting a couple of hundred dollars a month into a property is nothing. Of course, this changes when you own a dozen properties and they're all alligators.

For others, putting $500 or even $1000 a month into one property is doable, at least for a short while.

No matter how big or small your alligator, over time you'll get tired of it's nipping at you. For one thing, it can significantly reduce your profit. Each time you put money into the property after your initial investment, your rate of return goes down.

Another thing is the annoyance factor. Even if it's only $50 a month, you'll mentally begin to see the property as a liability instead of an asset. Remember, your profits, until you sell, are on paper. However, your losses each month are in cash.

Successful real estate investors look for cash cows and avoid alligators. The problem, of course, is finding such properties.

Today, prices have gone so high that by the time you finance the property with little or no cash and account for the other monthly costs, it's hard (but not impossible) to find a property that will bring in enough rent to give you a breakeven. Of course, rental rates in some areas have skyrocketed, which has helped enormously in creating cash cows. But even so, the challenge is in finding properties that are priced well enough to make sense as investments when putting little or no cash down.

It's a nitty-gritty challenge, one that every investor who wants to be wealthy must successfully face. The important thing about alligators, however, is that you can avoid them. By carefully selecting properties, you can get those that will either break even or be a cash cow (show a positive return). We'll go into this in great detail in Chapter 6, but first let's see the other problem of real estate investing.

Transaction Costs

The other concern with real estate investing is the cost of transactions. Real estate has one of the highest transaction costs of any investment. (One area that's often higher is rarities—rare paintings, coins, and other art objects.)

Assuming that you use an agent to both buy and sell a property (and pay full commission), your transaction costs will run you around 8 to 10 percent for the full trip (going and coming—buying and selling). On a $300,000 property, that means about $24,000 to $30,000.

Thus, although we said earlier that your profit on paper the first year might be $15,000, if you sell within a year, you would stand to lose all of the profit and all of your investment just in paying the transaction costs! You'd have to hold the property for at least two years before you could even hope to recoup your investment and three years before you'd actually start making any money.

It's easy to see why transaction costs, sometimes referred to as the hidden peril of real estate, are such a big deal. They can turn a wonderful investment into a money pit.

Not to worry, however. Remember that I said "if you pay the full transaction costs." There are ways around this, including getting no-cost financing, selling by owner, and having the other party pick up all or part of your costs. In other words, there are ways of getting your transaction costs reduced or eliminated entirely. We'll look into these in detail in Chapter 5.

TRAP

Partly because of transaction costs and partly because it's hard to always find a buyer when you want one, real estate should not be considered a liquid investment. Unlike stocks and bonds, you can't count on getting in and—especially—getting out quickly. Real estate by its very nature tends to be a long-term investment.

In for the Long Haul

Although it is possible to "flip," buy/control a property and quickly resell it, that type of investing is rare. Never mind the so-called gurus who claim you can get rich quick by flipping. It isn't going to happen that often.

That's not to say that at various times in hot markets flipping opportunities don't come up. They do and any savvy investor will take advantage of them. But I've been following the real estate market since the 1950s (when my dad was a broker/investor), and I can honestly tell you that for every 10 good long-term investment properties I found, I've located one that could be flipped. (And for every one good investment property, I'd often find 10 others that needed to be turned away!) (See Chapter 8 on flipping.)

All of which brings us to the final tenet of investing in real estate, the rule that will make you hugely successful, or, if violated, will cost you dearly: *Real estate is long-term investing.*

TIP

Any time you buy an investment property, you should have a holding horizon of at least 7 to 10 years. You should plan on keeping it that long before being able to sell for a big profit. Of course, if you should get lucky and have the opportunity to flip it quickly, by all means do so.

If you plan on long-term investing and buy properties wisely, even with little to no cash, it's hard to see how you can go wrong. Indeed, most of the "average" people in this country who are millionaires got to be that way by doggedly buying and holding (and occasionally selling for profit) real estate, specifically single-family homes. As I noted earlier, it's the American way to wealth!

In the next chapter we'll look at creating a plan for your success in real estate investing.

2

Creating Your Own Investment Road Map

I don't know about you, but when I want to get from where I am to someplace new to me, I get a map. I see the route that someone else has taken, and I follow it. On the computer, I go to a site like mapquest.com and get printed instructions. Or I drop over to the local AAA® and get one of their detailed maps. After all, if I don't have a map and I've never been there before, how will I find the place?

The same thing holds true with real estate investing. If you're just starting out, if this is your first or even second investment, you probably don't have a clear idea of how to get where you want to go. Of course, your ultimate destination may be perfectly clear to you—you want to be as wealthy as Getty; you want to own many cash-producing properties, be a landlord king! It's a common dream. But how do you get there?

If you've got little to no cash to invest, how do you get from where you are to where you want to be? The answer, obviously, is that you need a real estate road map. You need to learn the route from others. That's what you're going to get in this chapter.

What Should You Invest In?

After reading Chapter 1, I'm going to assume you're sold on investing in real estate. However, having said that, I'm sure you also realize that there are a lot of options. Here are some of the types of real estate you can invest in:

Your Real Estate Investing Opportunities

- Commercial buildings—a small strip mall to start
- Apartment houses—perhaps a fourplex to begin
- Industrial—a small manufacturing building at first
- Duplexes—a duet or double-unit rental
- **Single-family home or condo—one house/condo**
- Bare land—a vacation lot to start

These are just some of your options. Additionally, you could invest in an office building, or buy a tract of land and subdivide, or do something else. Your options in real estate are almost unlimited.

However, you'll notice that I've emphasized the single-family home/condo. Out of all your other options, this is where I suggest you do start for two very important reasons.

Reason Number One

I'm assuming you don't have a lot of experience in real estate. If that's the case, then single-family homes/condos is usually the safest and easiest area in which to gain knowledge. By dealing with just one unit, by learning to handle one tenant, by seeing how profits are made on a single property, you can quickly increase your knowledge base (both of how things are done and, even more important, of what you, yourself, are capable) with relatively little risk.

Reason Number Two

It's the road with the smallest cash investment. Home ownership is the United States' biggest business. There are well over 65 million single-family units in this country. In any one year about 10 percent of those are bought and sold. What this means is that there is an entire industry out there dedicated to financing single-family home sales. No other area of real estate can claim this.

In fact, never in the history of this country (or of the world, for that matter) has it been easier to purchase a single-family home/condo. Lenders, in fact, are dying to give you the money to buy them. Of course, this wasn't always the case.

Twenty-five years ago, the rule was that you needed 20 percent down to make the purchase. Institutional lenders like banks rarely would lend you more than 80 percent of the price (LTV stands for loan-to-value). Today, it's a different world. Institutional lenders are eager to offer 90 percent loans. In many cases they'll go as high as 95 percent. In a few cases, they'll go 100 percent, sometimes even 103 percent of the price!

Consider what that means to you. Instead of needing 20 percent down, you may be able to buy with only 10 percent down. Sometimes as little as 5 or even zero percent down. In some cases you can even get the lender to pay for your closing costs!

Different LTVs and Down Payments on a $300,000 Property

LTV	Down Payment	Cash Required for Down Payment
80%	20%	$60,000
90%	10%	30,000
95%	5%	15,000
100%	0%	0

You can put this kind of financing up against any other area of real estate, and you'll find there's no comparison. If you're buying commercial, industrial, apartment, or whatever, you're typically going to need 20 percent down, at minimum. If you try buying bare land, you'll probably find you need anywhere from 50 percent to 100 percent in cash.

Also, compare this to stocks, bonds, and hard assets like gold and silver. Again, you'll find there's no comparison. No other investment area offers you as high an LTV as a single-family property. No other investment area allows you to get in with so little of your money.

TIP

The name of the game in real estate investing is OPM— "other people's money." As long as you use OPM, you can control large investments with very little of YM, "your money."

Is it any wonder that I've emphasized single-family homes/condos? This is the road I suggest you begin to travel. (Note: I'm not saying that there aren't restrictions or that it doesn't require some effort. We'll begin to see how to acquire rentals with little-to-no-cash financing in the next chapter.)

Building the Road Map

Okay, you're willing to consider single-family homes as the road to follow, to carry you from where you are to real estate wealth. But now you need a vehicle to carry you along that road.

The vehicle I'm suggesting you use is called *sequential investing*, or sometimes, *serial investing*. (Serial is not to be confused with a box of breakfast food, or a serial killer, which are, of course, entirely different.)

Put as simply as possible, what I'm suggesting is that you consider the sequential (or serial) buying of homes. In other words, buy one house or condo. Keep it for awhile. Then buy another and hang onto it. After some time passes, buy a third, then a fourth, and so on. If you diligently keep driving this vehicle on the path I've indicated, how many properties do you think you can accumulate over 20 years? How much do you think they'll be worth?

TIP

Don't be afraid of condos. Yes, they may be harder to rent out because of restrictions imposed by home owners' associations, but new laws are liberalizing this. And in recent years the price appreciation of condos has equaled or even exceeded that of single-family homes.

Let's consider the first home. And let's say that instead of buying your first home today, you bought it 20 years ago. Further say that it cost you little or no cash to make the purchase.

If you bought the average price home (not condo—the figures are different for each) in the United States in 1984, you paid $86,000. If you kept it until 2004, that average priced home is worth roughly $225,000. Your profit (on paper) is $139,000. Further, during that time your tenants have been paying rent, which you've used to pay down the mortgage. After 20 years, it's roughly half of the original amount. Today you only owe around $46,000. That's another $40,000 that goes into the profit column. In other words, after putting little to nothing into this property, it has turned you a tidy profit of around $180,000.

What if instead of one house, you bought one every 2 years for 20 years? In 1986 you bought your second home. You paid $89,300 (the average price back then). Again, today it's also worth roughly $225,000. Your profit on paper is about $136,000. When you add in equity return from tenants paying off your mortgage, that goes up to about $175,000. With two homes you now have a net worth of roughly $355,000.

Let's say that two years later you bought another home. And another home after two more years. And so on. Today, you have 10 houses.

Granted, as time moved on you'd have paid more for each house. And your later equity and mortgage reduction is less. But even so, your profits in each still would have grown. Over the last 20 years there's no reason why your net worth couldn't exceed at least a million dollars. Again, this is with little or no cash down.

Does It Really Work That Way?

What I've done here is present the method, the road map. It's not complicated. You don't need to be a mathematical genius, lucky, or even a real estate agent to travel the path to financial success. You don't need a lot of cash. You do, however, need to get started and buy that first house. And you have to believe that over time real estate values will go up.

On the other hand, I've not shown you the difficulties that you could encounter along the way (some of which we discussed in the last chapter). These include the following:

Potential Difficulties with Sequential Investing

- You may not be able to buy lots of homes with little or no cash.
- You may have trouble finding suitable properties.
- You may find that the cash flow on one or more of your properties is too negative to make it/them worthwhile.

- A local or national recession or depression could cause you to lose properties.
- You may not like or want to be a landlord.
- You simply may not have the energy or desire to do it, given your family situation.

These difficulties are real. However, with the exception of your own personal limitations (such as not wanting to collect rent or not wanting to spend the time finding investment homes), most can be overcome as we'll see in subsequent chapters.

The Bottom Line

Ask yourself these questions:

- What am I going to be doing over the next 20 years that's better than becoming a successful real estate investor?
- Aren't I going to need a place to live? (So, why not buy a home to live in with an eye toward investment?)
- Aren't I going to have some spare time. (So, why not spend it buying up rental homes/condos?)

Remember, if you make a million dollars some other way, terrific! But if not, you will always have your property to fall back upon.

3
Little to No Cash Down Payment Financing

Everyone knows, or should know, that the key to buying real estate is getting the right financing. We've talked about this in the previous chapter as OPM, "other people's money." If you can get enough OPM, you can buy anything, even the Empire State Building.

TIP

Today there's a lot of OPM out there if you know where to look for it and how to get it.

In this chapter we'll cover OPM from institutional lenders (banks, mortgage bankers, and others). In the next chapter we'll talk about a different kind of OPM—getting it from the seller.

Lender's Resistance

At the onset, it's important to understand that lenders are basically hesitant to loan money to investors. The reason is simply that they are concerned about the risk. They are fearful that if things don't work out as you hoped after you buy a property, you will simply walk away from it (even though this will adversely affect your credit rating).

They understand that you don't have the emotional attachment to it that an owner/occupant may have. For you, it's strictly business. And, if you walk away, the lenders are stuck with the property.

Since lenders normally don't want to own property—they are strictly in the business of offering mortgages—they are reluctant to offer investor financing. At least in the past.

In recent years, however, if you have good credit and enough income to satisfy a lender, lenders will offer you, as an investor, a loan on just about any piece of real estate (with the possible exception of bare land). The problem is that they will limit their risk exposure by insisting that you put in some of your own money.

Today, if you are an investor, lenders want you to put in 20 percent of the price of the property and they will loan 80 percent. However, if you have very good credit, you may find a lender who's willing to accept only about 10 percent of your money down and put up 90 percent providing you're buying a single-family home or condo. The better financing on these is available because they are so easily resold in the event of a foreclosure and because you have better credit, thus reducing the lender's risk.

What this means is that if the price of the property is $300,000, the lender is going to want you, the investor, to put down at least 10 percent or $30,000 (plus closing costs, which we'll deal with in Chapter 5.) The lender will put up 90 percent or $270,000. In the trade this is called the lender's LTV or loan-to-value.

Getting a property that costs $300,000 for only 10 percent down is a pretty good deal, unless you don't happen to have $30,000 in the bank or don't have outstanding credit. If you don't and you still want to buy, then you need to change the parameters of your search.

How Do I Get a No-Down Mortgage When I Buy?

The simple truth of the matter is that if you're buying strictly for investment, you probably can't get a no-down mortgage from an institutional lender such as a bank. They won't lend to you on this basis simply because they are afraid, as previously noted, that you might skip out if times get tough. They want you to put enough of your money into it to assure you will keep making the payments on the property.

TRAP

Lenders don't particularly like investors—they love owner/occupant buyers.

On the other hand, this all changes if you're not an investor, but instead are buying to live in the property yourself—if you plan on being an owner-occupant. Over the past 30 years a great many studies have been done on the performance of owner-occupants of single-family homes and condos, and these have shown that owner-occupants, provided they have the right credit and income profile at the onset, are relatively risk free. They do have an emotional attachment to the property that will make them fight through thick and thin to hang on to it.

Further, up to a loan amount that is currently $333,700, these mortgages can be underwritten (a kind of guarantee) by the two huge secondary lenders in the United States: Freddie Mac and Fannie Mae. This means that the bank that initially loans the money has almost no risk exposure.

The result is that those who buy to live in the home can get LTVs as high as 95 percent. In some cases LTVs will go to 100 percent, and rarely to as high as 103 percent! In short, if you buy to live in the single-family home, you can get no-down financing (provided you have the appropriate income and credit score, as we'll get into shortly).

The Importance of Being Earnest

The great temptation for investors, then, is to say they will live in the property in order to get the good financing, and then not actually move in. By so doing they take advantage of better financing than they could get as investors. The reason for not moving in, of course, is that they may already have a house in which they live and they don't want to lose even a month's worth of rent from the property they are buying.

TRAP

It's important to understand here that we're not talking about pretending to be an owner-occupant. I do
not mean that you buy the property by telling the
lender that you're going to move in and then never do
so, renting out the property instead. Here we're talking about actually moving into the home and living
there for some time—occupying it.

No matter what you call this, it's simple lying, and if you do it, it
could land you in real hot water. Lenders are on the alert for people who say they are moving in when really they intend to rent out
the property. To confirm that you've moved in, a lender may call
on the phone after a month or two to check. Or a lender may send
your payment books to your attention at the new home's address
with no forwarding requested. Or a lender may even send someone by three or six months later to see how you're doing. If a tenant answers the door, the ruse is up.

Almost all mortgages are in some way insured, guaranteed, or
resold through government or quasigovernment agencies. That
means that if you lied and are caught, you will have to do a lot of
explaining to the Treasury Department. Penalties could be anything
from a demand to immediately repay the full amount of the loan to
indictment on criminal charges.

All of which is to tell you that if you're going to write down that
you intend to occupy the property, be sure you do in fact intend to
do that. Later on, after you've lived there for a while, perhaps a year
or two, you can think about converting it to a rental.

Becoming a Home Owner/Investor

But, doesn't this put a crimp in your efforts to invest in real estate
and to become a great realty entrepreneur? Buying a home to live
in hardly sounds like investing, does it?

Yes . . . and no.

There are two ways to look at investing in real estate. The first is
as a full-time proposition. You're out there 24/7 finding properties,

buying them, renting them, selling them. You're a regular Donald Trump, a wheeler and dealer in property.

The other way is as a part-time investor. Here you keep your regular day job and work at real estate in your off hours and on weekends. You buy a home and live in it for a few years; then you rent it out and buy another home to live in. Now you've got yourself a rental. In a few years you do it again.

Interestingly, although there are few people out there of the caliber of Trump, there are hundreds of thousands who have made their money slowly the part-time way. It's a simple of case of the turtle and the hare. Being a turtle can mean that you'll ultimately win the race.

TIP

You have to live somewhere, don't you? So why not buy a home to live in?

After living in the property for two years or so, convert it to a rental and buy another home to live in. In this way you can take advantage of the best real estate financing on the planet . . . and build a huge net worth. As noted in Chapter 2, it's called *sequential investing*.

The Fine Art of Sequential Investing

The idea here is really quite simple. You acquire properties (starting with single-family homes or condos) slowly, one at a time, living in each. You buy to live in them, but you rarely sell. Over time you acquire a vast holding in real estate.

Perhaps you know someone who has done this (many people have). Typically they lead quiet lives and are not ostentatious. You may have several in your own neighborhood. Many have regular jobs; but after a few years when rental incomes begin to increase, they devote a few hours a week to taking care of their properties and relax the rest of the time. They are most busy at the first of the month when they go around "harvesting." That is, collecting their rents.

Over the long haul, the mortgages on these properties get paid off. When they are originally purchased, the mortgage may be very high; as noted before, it is often 95 percent of the purchase price or more (offered because these investors typically first lived in the properties they bought for a time before converting them to rentals, thus qualifying for the high loan-to-value mortgage). However, over 30 years that mortgage gets reduced eventually to zero. At the same time, normal inflation pushes the rental income up. Over time the amount the investor pays on the mortgage gets whittled away while the income it produces climbs. More and more of the rental money ends up in the investor's pocket.

Some investors have a dozen properties. Others have many, many more. Of course, once they acquire a large number, they can refinance to take out money and buy properties strictly as investments, without living in them. And, as their properties grow they tend to hire good property management firms to take care of the rentals, so they have even more time off for themselves.

Most such investors I know tend to keep around a dozen such properties—and they take care of them by themselves. This is probably the most manageable amount.

TIP

A dozen paid off properties bringing in an average of $1500 a month provide $18,000—not a bad monthly income. Twelve paid-off properties with an average price of $250,000 comes to $3 million, again not a bad net worth.

Remember, the principle is simple—you begin by buying properties to live in. Later you convert and rent them out to make the payments. Eventually they pay themselves off, and you live off the income they generate. It's sort of like the grand old game of Monopoly.

Sequential investing appeals to many people because of its simplicity. You don't have to be a genius to make it work. Indeed, all you need do is keep your eyes open for good properties and purchase them as you can.

TRAP

Some mortgage documents specify that you cannot rent out the property you originally buy and occupy. I have not heard of a case where this was invoked and it may or may not be enforceable. Nevertheless, it's something to watch out for.

Not a "Get Rich Quick" Scheme

Remember, this is not a get rich quick scheme. When you get started, there will be little to no cash flow from the properties. On the other hand, you'll be putting little to nothing into them. They will be like little plants that require nurturing. You may have some out-of-pocket expenses that go to pay for maintenance and repair . . . and occasionally you may have to offset some mortgage and tax payments.

Of course, you probably will get some immediate tax relief once you convert the properties to rentals as interest, taxes, maintenance, and other costs may be deductible (see Chapter 12 on taxation issues). It is for this reason that you should plan on continuing with your day job, at least for awhile. (Keep in mind that even while you're living in your home as an owner-occupant, you should be able to deduct property taxes and mortgage interest up to high limits, which is why any kind of home ownership tends to be a good deal.)

What If I'm Not a Young Investor?

You're 50, 60, or even 70 years old. Is it too late for you to get on the real estate gravy train?

Not at all. Age is not normally a consideration with lenders. They are more than happy to give a 70-year-old a 30-year loan (if he or she has the proper credit and income), even though that person's life expectancy may be only 5 or 10 years.

However, unlike those who are younger and can afford to make a few mistakes along the way, the more mature you are, the more careful you need to be. If you're more mature and are seeking to get started investing in real estate, be scrupulously careful about what you buy. Only purchase in areas where prices are rapidly appreciating, where there's a strong tenant base, and where you can afford to get in without straining your finances (even if this means moving to a different area).

Further, you will want to spend more of your time hunting for "flippables." These are properties you can buy or tie up and quickly resell. (See Chapter 8.)

Be especially carefully not to spend money that you have set aside for your retirement. Remember, no investment is risk free. You should only take risks with money you can afford to lose.

How Do You Take Your Profits?

It's all well and good to buy more and more property. But, how do you get money out of it? Everyone knows that real estate is nonliquid—it's hard to cash out.

Real estate is only hard to cash out if you try to sell above the market. Sell at or just below market, and you can move any property in almost any market. Time your sale to coincide with an upswing of the realty market (such as happened in the first half decade of this century), and you can make huge profits as well as sell quickly.

TIP

You don't necessarily need to sell to get your money out.

Two things happen as you own a property over time. The first is that prices go up. This is a function of supply and demand as well as inflation. Buy a property, hold it for five years, and chances are it will be worth considerably more than you paid for it (assuming you didn't happen to buy at the beginning of the down cycle).

The other thing is that your mortgage balance usually goes down (unless you have a rare interest-only loan), albeit slowly. Each month as you make that payment, a small amount of money is returned to equity. During the first 10 years of ownership, that amount tends to be small. But, after the tenth year, it accelerates until by the twenty-fifth year, almost the entire payment is going back to equity (assuming a 30-year mortgage).

All of this means that just by keeping the property, your equity grows each year. And after a while, you can "harvest" this equity by refinancing. For example, if you bought a property for $200,000 with a $195,000 mortgage and that property goes up in price to $300,000, you've now got $105,000 in equity all because of price appreciation. At the same time if the mortgage goes down to $170,000, your equity is now boosted an additional $25,000 because of equity return. You have a total of $130,000 of equity to play with.

A few years ago lenders frowned on giving cash-out mortgages to investors. Indeed, the most you were likely to get was a 70 percent mortgage. If you got anything higher, the proceeds had to go to pay off the existing mortgage and costs. Cash-outs seldom were allowed.

Today that's changed. Many of today's lenders will allow a cash-out to you on an 80 percent LTV mortgage, in some few cases as high as a 90 percent mortgage. (Shop around with the help of a good mortgage broker to find these loans.)

What this means is that when you refinance to an 80 percent mortgage on a $300,000 property, you could get an LTV (loan-to-value) of $240,000. Since you only owe $170,000, you'd net $70,000 *in cash* before any refinancing (refi) charges. With a 90 percent LTV refi, that's $100,000 cash out to you, quite a nice harvest! (Of course, you may be asked to pay a stiffer interest rate and more points and need more income to qualify. But at least the cash-out refinancing is there.)

An alternative method of getting your money out is to get a second mortgage. Many banks happily offer these to anyone who qualifies, including investors. Generally speaking, the CLTV (combined loan-to-value, a new term to remember) is the same as for a large first mortgage—80 percent and rarely as high as 90 percent. However, the higher interest rate and points are only on the second mortgage. When this is paired with a lower interest rate existing first, the combined interest rate can be lower than for a single large new refi mortgage.

There are also private sources of secondary financing for lenders. These are investors who will give you cash out. However, they tend to charge much higher interest rates, and the loans tend to be for a much shorter term.

Finally, keep in mind that because you're only refinancing and not changing title, there are no immediate tax consequences of taking the money out. Indeed, as long as you hold the property, there won't be. Thus, you can do anything you want with the money you cash out, including using it to buy another home! (There may, however, be significant taxes to pay if and when you eventually sell. See Chapter 12.)

Buy one property, hold it for a few years, get cash out, and buy another home. Now you've got two. Hold them for a few years, get cash out, and buy another. Now you've got three. Keep repeating the process, and it won't be too many years before you yourself are a land baron!

There's a big trap here. In order to refinance, you must show income. This is another reason, at least in the early years, to keep your day job!

Are There Any Drawbacks?

Is this plan obvious? When I first explain the concept of sequential investing to people, they often remark that it's so easy . . . why didn't they think of it? Indeed, it is obvious and so simple that it works. However, there are some potential pitfalls that you should be aware of.

The first is that this plan depends on the financing. You must plan to live in the property to get these little-to-no-cash loans. That means that every couple of years you'll be uprooting your family and moving to another house. That probably means new schools for the kids and new friends in the neighborhood for you. It's a sacrifice that you must be willing to make.

The second is that it works best over time. If you start early on, then you have years to acquire the properties. If you wait until you're near retirement age, you will still be able to acquire a number of properties, but you will find that at least initially you're going to need to nurture these young ventures just when you want to get money out to retire. For those nearing retirement age, a better plan may be to also look for properties you can buy and quickly resell for a profit, as described in Chapter 8.

The third is that this works best, at least initially, if you have a stable job. You need to stay in one area for around 10 years or so in order to grow your stable of homes. Don't even attempt this if you plan on moving around the country a lot. The last thing you want are houses in different parts of the country. The only way you can manage them properly, as we'll see in Chapter 10, is if they are located nearby. Trying to landlord a house in Maine when you currently reside in Oregon is like trying to weave spaghetti—not impossible, but very, very difficult to do.

Where Do I Find a Lender?

This part, at least, is easy. Today, lenders are everywhere. You can go to a bank, but it's much easier to go to a mortgage broker. (Similarly, to buy stock you could go to an individual company, but it's much easier to go to a stockbroker.)

Like a stockbroker, a mortgage broker handles loans from a wide variety of lenders, some within your state and some from across the country. Usually the mortgage broker can tailor the loan just to fit your needs depending on your income, credit, and assets.

TRAP

Don't give up before you start. Many people assume that just because they have little to no cash, iffy credit, and a low income, there's no way they can buy any property. It's not true. Almost anyone can get financing today. Don't stop looking for an institutional loan until at least four separate mortgage brokers have firmly said no.

Today, institutional loans are available for nearly all people. It's just that if you've got problems in qualifying, you might get charged a higher interest rate, be required to put more money down, or need to get someone with better credit to go in on the loan with you.

Mortgage brokers are listed as such in the yellow pages. Lenders are banks, savings and loans, credit unions, mortgage bankers, and so on. Although these are all easy to find, you are probably best off with a recommendation from a friend who's successfully used one or a real estate agent you trust.

Online mortgage companies seem to come and go, particularly since the collapse of the Internet craze a few years back. Check using a good search engine as well as examining some of the larger ones such as quicken.com, MSN.com, or eloan.com.

Can I Really Qualify for an Institutional Loan?

Today if you want an institutional loan such as we've been describing, it all depends on your profile. The term *profiling* has gotten a lot of bad press in recent years. However, keep in mind that here we're not talking about racial or ethnic profiling. Here it's strictly financial. It's using profiles created from a database to come up with borrowers who are likely to succeed and those who are likely to fail and fall into foreclosure. This computerized analysis can determine just how likely you are to keep making your monthly payments. It's also used to determine how big a monthly payment you can afford to make. And it will determine if you'll get the best interest rate, or a higher interest rate to compensate the lender for an increased risk.

Thus, the first step is to find out just what your profile looks like. You can do this easily enough by getting yourself off to a good mortgage broker (or going online to one of the many Web lenders) and getting "pre-approved."

Pre-approval is a process in which a lender takes a close look at your finances. The lender checks your income, your credit, and many of your expenses. You fill out a questionnaire of about 60 questions. The lender then feeds that information into a computer that has a database of over 300,000 successful and unsuccessful borrowers. It also does a preliminary credit check. And it spits out the maximum monthly payment you can afford to make as well as whether or not you can afford to buy a house and what the maximum price will be!

Whatever it says, you can take it to the bank . . . literally!

Be Careful to Get the Right Pre-Approval

While I'm touting pre-approval, it's important to understand that it's not without problems. It's important that you recognize these *before* you get pre-approved.

In the past, real estate agents would often "pre-qualify" their borrowers. They would ask you a few rather personal financial questions and then, from your responses, determine how big a payment you could afford and, from that, how big a house you could afford to purchase. Today, that almost never happens. Good agents will simply refer you to a lender or mortgage broker who will pre-approve you. When you come back with your pre-approval letter, both you and the agent know what you can afford. In truth, there's less need for the agent to know your detailed personal financial information than ever before.

Also, be sure to get underwriting approval. Underwriting is the process whereby secondary lenders (such as Fannie Mae or Freddie Mac) approve borrowers from primary lenders (such as your bank). Remember, the loan you get from your bank usually doesn't stay with your bank; it's sold on the secondary market. To be saleable, you the borrower must have underwriter approval. A good lender will have your application approved by an underwriter. Today this can be done electronically in a matter of minutes. Now the letter of pre-approval will state that the lender will *commit* to loan you funds based on a maximum monthly payment. This is the pre-approval that you can take to the bank.

Finally, be sure your approval includes a credit check.

Some mortgage brokers will simply get some information from you over the phone and then send you a pre-approval letter. This is *not* something to you can take to any bank I know of. The minimum requirement for pre-approval is a credit check. Today this is often done automatically as part of the "underwriting" process.

While mortgage brokers, individuals, or companies that broker loans for lenders are your best source for both financing and approval letters, beware. A pre-approval letter issued by just a mortgage broker may not be worth the paper it's written on. The reason is that mortgage brokers do *not* fund loans themselves. They only broker them. You want your pre-approval commitment letter to come from a lender, the one who actually makes the loan.

The Bottom Line

In this chapter we've looked at how to get little-to no-down institutional financing to buy a home that you initially live in and, over the long term, convert to a rental. We've examined the art of sequential investing.

However, this may not appeal to you. You may want something short term to make money quickly in real estate. If so, then check into Chapter 8 on flipping. In the next chapter we'll talk about another way to get into a property with little to no cash: have the seller handle the financing.

4

Get Others to Lend You the Money to Buy

You want to buy a rental property, but three things stop you:

- You have little or no cash.
- Your credit leaves much to be desired.
- You have less income than the banks are looking for.

You're out of luck, right? Not necessarily.

In the last chapter we saw how to get an institutional investor, such as a bank, to lend virtually all of the money you need to make the purchase—provided you agreed to live in the property. But what if you don't want to occupy the property? Or what if no institutional lender will offer financing because you can't meet their strict income and credit requirements? Can you still buy a rental with little or no cash?

Surprisingly, the answer is, "Yes, you can!" Some of the best financing for an investor actually comes from sellers and other sources. These sources often don't care whether or not you intend to occupy the property or rent it out. Indeed, many simply don't ask. Also, your credit and income are much less important.

Many sellers are eager to give buyers financing, often seeing this as a way to help make the deal. Others are looking for good loans. If you find a seller in these positions, you can get some very surprising and worthwhile financing deals.

There are two basic ways that a seller can finance your purchase of the property. The first is for the seller to lend you all the money. The second is for the seller to lend you only a portion and for you to assume the seller's existing financing, or to get new financing on your own.

When the Seller Owns the Home Free and Clear

Let's begin with a seller who owns her property free and clear. She has no mortgage and no financing of any kind on it. (Don't think this type of seller doesn't exist—nearly 25 percent of all home owners in this country don't have any mortgage on their property!)

The structure of the sale is fairly simple. Instead of going out to get a brand new mortgage, you say to the seller, "Will you give me a mortgage so I can purchase your property?"

You can *ask* for any LTV. For example, you might ask for an 80 percent mortgage from the seller with 20 percent down supplied by you. Or, if you have less cash, you might ask the seller for a 90 percent LTV with a 10 percent down payment from you. If you're really daring, you can ask the seller for a 100 percent LTV with nothing down from you. The seller essentially gives you the property, and you give the seller a mortgage for its full value.

Will sellers actually go along with such offers?

Sometimes. It depends on why they want to sell. The seller, for example, may be having trouble selling the property. He or she hopes that by offering the buyer (you) financing, there'll be a quicker sale. In this situation the seller often anticipates that the buyer will have some credit problems (or else why wouldn't the buyer get institutional financing?) and is prepared to accept this. Thus, if you can't get an institutional loan for one reason or another, this becomes a good alternative. In fact, many very successful investors *only* buy property when they can get seller financing.

Other sellers are looking to invest their money in a bondlike vehicle that will pay them a high interest rate. This is particularly the case with older sellers who plan to live on the money they receive from their property. If you give them cash, they'll just stick the money in the bank or a CD and collect the interest. In today's market, however, that's only a few percent. However, a mortgage typically pays interest that is several percent greater, so they may be thrilled if you'll give them a mortgage paying the higher rate.

Keep in mind, however, that sellers are mindful of protecting their interest in the property. The home may be their largest single investment and, as we've said, they are counting on the money from it to live on, perhaps in retirement. Therefore, sellers are increasingly reluctant to offer you complete financing, which puts them at greater risk. The smaller the amount of your money you are willing to sink into the property, the less likely you are to get seller financing. Putting at least some money in (even just 5 percent) helps a lot.

What this comes down to in the actual negotiations is something like this: For every seller who's willing to give a full mortgage when you put 20 percent down, there are probably only half as many who are willing to give a full loan when you put only 10 percent down. Cut that number to 5 percent down, and you probably eliminate half of the remainder. Try to get nothing down, and you probably eliminate another 50 percent. No, it's not impossible. It just means you've got to look longer and harder.

TIP

The more of your own money that you can pour into the deal, the better your chances of getting the seller to lend you money to buy. The less of your own money that you put in, the less are the chances the seller will go along with you.

When the Seller Owes Money on the Property

Not all sellers are in a position to handle all of the financing for you. After all, if the sellers are themselves up to their ears in mortgages, they simply don't have much equity to convert into a loan for you.

In theory any seller can offer you financing by simply giving you a mortgage for his or her entire equity in a property. For example, a seller may be offering a home for $200,000 and have an existing mortgage for $150,000. If the seller offers you a second mortgage for $50,000, suddenly you've got all the money to make the purchase. (The $150,000 existing mortgage plus the seller's second mortgage of $50,000 adds up to the $200,000 asking price.)

There's just one hiccup—that existing first mortgage. In order to make the deal we just described, you very likely would have to "assume" or take over the obligation of repaying that loan. In order to do that, however, you'd need lender approval. And the fact of the matter is that in today's world, the chances are slim to none that you'd get it.

TRAP

Today lenders don't want to let new buyers assume the existing financing. Or, if they do, they want the new buyers to qualify just as if the buyers were applying for a brand new loan.

Thus, you're faced with a new alternative: get part of the purchase price (enough to cover the seller's existing financing) from an institutional lender (bank), and get the rest of the financing from the seller, usually in the form of a second mortgage.

"But," you may be saying, "I couldn't get institutional financing before. In fact, that's the reason I'm looking at seller financing. How can I get it now?"

The answer is that before you were trying to obtain 100 percent (or close to it) institutional financing. Now, you're going for much, much less. In our above example, let's say you got a new loan to replace the seller's existing loan of $150,000. On a $200,000 property that's only a 75 percent LTV. It's oh so much easier to qualify for a 75 percent LTV than for a 95 or 100 percent LTV. Your credit doesn't have to be spotless, your income not nearly so high and, perhaps best of all, you probably won't be required to live in the property!

Thus, your offer would be for part new financing (which you would secure from an institutional lender through a mortgage broker) and part seller financing (which the seller would give to you). This combination can often be much easier to obtain than either a large institutional loan or a large seller loan.

TRAP

Institutional lenders are aware of investors who are securing just the sort of financing noted above. While, at least in theory, they should not be concerned since their exposure is only limited to, in our example, 75 percent of the purchase price, nevertheless, in an effort to avoid any threat of unpleasantness whatsoever (such as a foreclosure in the event the investor fails to meet his or her obligations), some lenders are now considering **CLTV.**

CLTV stands for combined loan-to-value. In other words, in qualifying you for the 75 percent mortgage, a lender may also take into account the second mortgage the seller is providing. If the seller happens to be offering a 25 percent second mortgage, that means that your CLTV is 100 percent. When that's the case, these lenders will pull back and refuse to loan.

To me it makes no sense since, regardless of how much money you put into the property or how large a mortgage the seller gives you, the only thing a lender should be concerned with is its own LTV. Nevertheless, lenders who worry about CLTV will make it more difficult for you to get combined institutional/seller financing.

The solution?

Look for a lender that doesn't worry about CLTV. I suggest that you be up front with your mortgage broker (MB) and explain the deal in all its details. Chances are the MB will be able to direct you to a more appropriate lender.

How Do I Make a "Seller Financing" Offer?

Seller financing is done at the time you make your purchase offer. Instead of putting into the purchase offer a standard contingency that the sale is subject to your obtaining a new mortgage from an institutional lender, you put in that the sale is subject to the seller's giving you financing. (If you're doing a combined financing—institutional and seller—you would list the terms of both loans.)

For the seller's mortgage, you include the desired interest rate, points (usually none), term, and so forth. In other words, you make the deal contingent upon the seller's agreeing to financing. If the seller won't give it to you, there's no deal. It's time to move on and look for a more amenable seller. However, if you make the price good enough, any seller will at least seriously consider the offer.

In today's market, it's true that most sellers are intent on getting cash out. Frequently they need the money to plunk down on the next house they are buying. However, as we've seen, occasionally you'll come across a seller who has other plans for the equity. Then seller financing is possible. Just keep in mind that, unlike with cash offers, you may need to make many offers on many houses before you find a seller who is agreeable.

What If the Seller Wants to Approve My Credit?

As noted, the beauty of seller financing is that there is no formal qualifying. However, most sellers will want to be at least assured that you have the wherewithal to make the mortgage payments. (Any good real estate agent will insist that you demonstrate this.)

Therefore, there's typically a credit report run and sometimes income verification (where your employer confirms your employment longevity and salary) and deposit verification (where your bank confirms how much money you have on hand) are performed. These can be handled by most agents.

It's then up to the seller to determine if you're worthy enough to buy the property and to be given seller financing. However, unlike with institutional lenders, there's no computer scoring or other arcane techniques. Rather, it's just a seller's guess. And the more anxious sellers are to get rid of the property, the more likely they are to accept less then sterling qualifications on your part.

What Are Other Types of Financing?

TIP

The first rule in real estate is that everything is negotiable, and the second rule is that creativity pays. There are all sorts of other types of financing available.

All kinds of financing are available. For example, I've seen family (shared) financing.

Shared Financing

In these circumstances a son or daughter may want to buy an investment house. He or she has the income to handle it, but not the cash. So the parents pop for the down payment and closing costs. Then they share ownership. Typically the son or daughter will handle property management and, when it's time to sell, the profits will be split up.

This system, of course, is not limited to families. It will work with friends, buddies, or even perfect strangers. However, a word of caution: Put it into writing.

People, even friends and close relatives, often forget what was said months or years earlier. When it's time to sell, you want to have in writing exactly how the profits (or if something goes wrong, the losses) are split up. Further, you want to be sure that there are solid escape clauses allowing you, or another party, to exit the deal if situations change. (For example, you could lose your job or your sibling, friend, or son or daughter could need to move out of the area.)

All of which is to say that if you intend doing any type of shared financing, spend the bucks to have a good attorney draw up a rock solid agreement. It won't cost that much and it could save lots of hassle and money later on.

The tax advantages of property ownership (deduction of taxes, interest, and other expenses on investment property) can be divided up in many different ways among shared owners. If this is of interest to you, check in advance with your accountant or tax attorney.

Loans Based on Your Assets

Yet another type of financing that is available is borrowing not on the property you are buying, but on other property. The easiest way to conceive of this is to borrow on stocks or bonds that you own. Very low interest rate loans are available, often through stock brokers and banks. You can then use this money to purchase new property.

Another method frequently used by experienced real estate investors is to refinance property they already own in order to make a new purchase. For example, you may have three rental homes in which you have substantial equity. You now refinance these (either with individual loans or with a blanket loan, which covers all three) and use the funds to buy a fourth house. If you've ever played the game Monopoly you know the basics of how this works.

Borrowing on owned property is a great way to obtain financing because you can get the mortgage set up before you start out looking for the new property to be acquired. Then, once you've got the money in hand, you're suddenly a cash buyer. You can make all-cash offers on homes and sometimes get surprisingly good prices because of it.

You get financing on your existing properties in the same way you would if you were obtaining a new mortgage. You go to a mortgage broker and explain which properties you have to offer. Your broker can then suggest whether to get separate loans on all of them (assuming there's more than one) or a single combined loan.

TIP

A blanket loan that covers more than one property is sometimes easier to obtain. But, if times go bad with one property and you can't make the payments, you could lose all of the homes covered under the loan.

Also, keep in mind that when you try to refinance existing property, lenders will not allow you to count all of your rental income, but they *will* insist that you count all of your expenses in calculating your ability to repay the loan. While this may seem patently unfair, the justification lenders make is that there will always be periods of high vacancy that no one counts on. They want to be sure you have the wherewithal to handle these. Therefore, you'll still usually need some outside income when you refinance.

TRAP

Another way to purchase from a seller with existing financing on the property is to buy "subject to" the loans. In this financing, you don't assume the responsibility for repayment—that continues to rest with the seller. You, however, agree to make the payments.

On the surface, buying "subject to" would seem to be an ideal way to buy. You get the existing financing without going through the hassle and expense of a refi. And at the same time, if things go bad and you need a clean exit, you simply walk away—remember, your name is not on the loan! (Of course, the seller and his or her attorney would have a few clear words to say about that, but that's a different story. See Appendix 4.)

Yes, it can look good from a certain perspective. However, look at it in a different way. If lenders, as we've discussed, don't want to let you assume existing mortgages, they most certainly don't want you to buy the property without telling them! They feel, with some justification, that this threatens their interest.

Therefore, lenders usually subscribe to a service that lets them know when a property on which they have a loan changes title. Thus, as soon as you record title in your name, they know the old owner has sold, but has not paid off the existing loans. Since these loans almost certainly contain a "due on sale" clause, lenders will usually immediately begin foreclosure to regain title to the property.

This almost certainly will panic any seller and, while you may be able to refinance your way out of it with a new loan, it could also cause you to lose whatever interest you have in the property.

How often does this worst case scenario happen? In talking to one loan broker who handled foreclosures, I was told that only in about three-fourths of the cases does the underlying lender learn about the "subject to" purchase and then foreclose, usually when the new buyer doesn't make the loan payments.

Beware of "Buy and Walk"

This leads to another issue. What about just buying a property for nothing down (we'll discuss closing costs in the next chapter), getting the loan "subject to," (as just described), renting the property out for awhile, not making any mortgage payments, and then simply walking away?

Can it be done? Yes.

Has it been done? Yes.

Should it be done? No.

First, there are ethical considerations. Usually in such nothing-down schemes, it's the seller who takes the bigger beating. The property title passes to a buyer who then financially rapes it, takes what money he or she can get for renting it for a few months before the lender(s) catches up, and then leaves. Now, to save whatever equity the seller originally had, he or she must go through an expensive foreclosure process, take the property back, and try to reinstate the original mortgage or, if that fails, refinance. Unfortunately, many sellers may not be able to qualify for a refi, meaning they'd lose all their interest in the property.

This is not something I'd want to have on my conscience, and I hope you wouldn't either.

Second, there's the practical side. These nothing-down schemes usually go bad fast. This means that the buyer often collects only a couple of months of rent before the world comes crashing down. As soon as the lender finds out what's happening, which is when the buyer doesn't make a payment, and the lender goes after the seller for the payment, the lender gets an order to attach the rent (which is usually another provision of mortgages). The rental income is diverted to the lender (or the seller), and the scheming buyer walks, perhaps with one to three months worth of rent.

Is it worth it? Remember, there's the hassle of negotiating a deal, of going through an escrow (not to mention the closing costs, as discussed in the next chapter), finding tenants, collecting rent, and so on. Further, some jurisdictions have ruled such schemes are illegal, meaning that there's the threat of criminal prosecution.

Thus, even if the ethical considerations aren't enough to deter a buyer, the practical considerations should be.

Land Contract of Sale— A Legal Alternative?

There is another alternative. Instead of buying the property outright and taking title, you obtain a "land contract of sale." (Although this was originally used primarily for land-only purchases, today it can be used for land and improvements, such as a house.) Under this type of contract, you enter into an agreement with the seller to purchase the property at a future date. In the meantime the seller continues to make payments on the existing financing, and you make payments to the seller that go toward paying off the lender's equity. When that equity is paid off, the seller issues you a deed and you refinance.

Easy?

Not really. Without the protection of a deed in your name initially and title insurance to back it up, the seller might just sell the same property to two different buyers or maybe 20 different buyers. How would you know? In this case, it's the seller who might have the scheme.

To avoid this, some buyers have their contract notarized and then attempt to have it recorded, thus giving notice that the property is being sold. Unfortunately, this can have the undesired effect of triggering the due-on-sale clause that the lender has. It can all end up in expensive litigation.

All of which is to say, be creative when you're considering lender financing. But don't get too creative!

TIP

If you have assets in a retirement account, you should consult with your financial adviser before converting them to cash. You may be counting on them for retirement or other uses, and you could be risking your financial future by borrowing against them.

Other Types of Little–to-No-Cash Financing

As noted, the types and sources of real estate financing for investors is limited only by your imagination. Don't feel boxed in by imagined rules. If you can come up with a creative idea, try it out on an agent and attorney, then in the field. It just might work.

For example, some people finance their real estate purchase (at least the down payment) with cash borrowed on credit cards. Is this a good way to buy property? No, it's not, because the interest rate on credit cards (often 20 percent or higher) will kill you in the long run. I've seen people who tried this creative approach, only to eventually lose their property to foreclosure.

On the other hand, as a short-term solution, it can work. If you need to borrow the money for a short period of time, say less than six months, and then have a plan to replace it with a permanent long-term loan, sure . . . it might very well work.

Be creative. But consider both the up side and the down side. And before taking action, talk it over with a financial adviser, such as a good real estate agent, tax attorney, or accountant.

5

The Big Surprise—
Transaction Costs

The down payment, at least when we're getting heavy financing as explained in the last few chapters, may turn out to be the least of your cash worries. For most new investors the hefty closing costs or, as these costs are more appropriately called, transaction costs are the big surprise.

In a typical real estate round-trip (buying and later selling a property), the transaction costs can easily amount to 10 percent of the value of the home. On a $200,000 home that's $20,000. On a $500,000 home it's $50,000 or more. These costs include:

Typical Transaction Costs

- The commission to the listing agent who eventually sells your home
- The points and fees for the loan when you purchase
- The costs of running an escrow and obtaining title insurance, possibly twice
- Attorney fees and other incidental costs
- Garbage fees that lenders, escrow agencies, and title insurance companies have become notorious for throwing in (a garbage fee is one that is unwarranted)

In the previous chapters we temporarily brushed aside these costs in order to make clear how the financing was structured. Now, however, we're going to deal directly with them.

TIP

If you're attempting to buy real estate and have little to no cash, you're definitely going to want to reduce or, when possible, eliminate your transaction costs.

Buy and Sell on Your Own

As we all know (or should know) the single biggest cost in a transaction is usually the commission. This is mainly a cost only for the seller, although it may be a cost for the buyer if a buyer's broker was used. However, if you eventually plan on selling the property you buy, it will be a cost for you.

While there is no "set rate" for a commission, today most agents charge between 5 and 6 percent. If the round-trip costs for a transaction are roughly 10 percent, very often 60 percent of that amount goes to the agent. On a $200,000 property that amounts to a $12,000 commission. On a $500,000 property it's a whopping $30,000 commission.

Obviously, the way to cut costs is to sell or buy without the services of an agent. There is nothing wrong with doing this. No one says you must use an agent to handle a transaction for you.

On the other hand, only a fool would wander into an uncharted wilderness without a guide. You don't want to be that fool when you first get started investing. It's very wise to rely on a good agent's experience when you're first getting your feet wet. In other words, pay the fees the first or second time. Then, once you see how it's done, you can try it yourself.

TRAP

There are many books out there that will help you sell a home on your own (including one that I wrote), and they should all tell you not to try it on your own on your first time out.

Once you've got a series of transactions under your belt, it's a different story. Now you've got the experience. Keep in mind, however, that while you may know you're competent to handle a real estate transaction, the other party you're dealing with may not. I've often seen situations where the seller is perfectly content to sell FSBO (by owner), but where the buyer insists that an agent handle the transaction. Further, the buyer insists that the seller pay that agent's fee, usually half a full commission or about 3 percent of the sales price.

You may complain loudly that you know what you're doing when acting on your own as a seller and there's no need for an agent. But the buyer may simply say, "No agent, no deal." So in this situation you get the agent and pay the fee—or look for another buyer.

Should You Get a Real Estate License?

Some investors get real estate licenses, and there can be some advantages. For example, as an agent and a Realtor® (member of the National Association of Realtors) you can sign up with your local real estate board and get the multiple listings. This can be a terrific help when you're scouting for properties, particularly if you can get them as they first come out. On the other hand, just about any real estate agent can give you at least limited access (and sometimes full access) to these same listings. And these listings are almost all readily available on the Internet at sites like realtor.com (although they tend to appear later than the paper listings.) So you can pretty much accomplish this without the benefit of a real estate license.

Further, as an agent you can claim a portion of the commission when you buy property. You can represent yourself and, at least in theory, get the buyer's agent's half (usually around 3 percent) of the purchase price. That can be a substantial amount of money (up to $6000 on a $200,000 transaction, $15,000 on a $500,000 purchase).

Further, as an agent, you may be able to claim as tax deductions many of your expenses during the ownership and renting of the property. These can add up to sizeable deductions.

So why not get that real estate license?

There are actually some downsides to having a license, unless you want to actually become an agent and sell property to others for a living. While there's nothing wrong with enrolling in a course that will teach you about real estate, the license itself can be a disadvantage.

One big reason is that lenders don't like to make their best loans to real estate agents. They know (or suspect) that agents are making creative deals, and they worry that what's stated on the purchase agreement, which is their guiding document, may not reflect the true deal. This is particularly the case when there's a commission going to the buyer of the home who also happens to be an agent. In short, agents usually get worse financing, if any at all.

Further, you will want to disclose to any seller that you hold an agent's license. This typically takes the form of a statement bold and clear on the purchase offer that states that the buyer (or seller) is a licensed real estate salesperson (or broker). If you're negotiating a tight deal, this sometimes is just enough to scare a seller away. (The reason you need to disclose your agent's license is to prevent the seller (or buyer) from later claiming that you had special knowledge and took unfair advantage. Some deals have been rescinded and damages awarded because agents failed to disclose their true status.)

TIP

My suggestion is that if you're going to invest, just be an investor. You usually don't need an agent's license. (Although, as noted, getting the agent's knowledge is very worthwhile.)

Getting the Other Party to Pay

What about the rest of the closing costs in a transaction? In real estate everything is negotiable. Normally, buyers pay their share and sellers pay theirs (as determined by local custom). However, there's nothing to say that you can't have the other party pay your closing costs (sometimes even including the agent's sales commission!).

Why would the other party be willing to do that? Actually, they wouldn't do it willingly or happily. If I'm selling my house and the buyers ask me to pay their closing costs, my answer is, "No, what a ridiculous question, case closed."

On the other hand, if the investors/buyers write into the purchase agreement a clause that says their purchase is contingent (subject to) my (the seller) paying the closing costs, then it's a little different.

Now the case is that if I want to sell, I have to pay their costs. If I don't pay their costs, then I chance losing the deal. The buyers here have made the closing costs a deal point (a deal maker or breaker).

Of course, if you as an investor/buyer demand something in one area, you're likely to have to give something up in another area. If you ask the sellers to pay your closing costs, chances are they will want you to pay a higher price. What you gain with one hand, you can lose with the other, right?

Not necessarily. Remember, as a buyer/investor it's highly unlikely you'll be going in at full price. More likely you'll low-ball the sellers hoping to pick up the property at a bargain price. All of which is to say that there's probably going to be a lot of negotiation before the final price is agreed upon.

When that's the case, my suggestion is that you do *not* bring up the matter of your closing costs. Rather, you bargain as ruggedly as you can for the price. If the sellers ultimately agree to your original low-ball figure, then forget about asking them to pay closing costs. You're already getting the house for a steal.

However, what if you don't have enough cash to handle the closing costs? Why not meet the seller's higher price but write into the deal that they must pay for your cash closing costs? In effect, you're giving them their price with one hand and taking it back in extra transaction fees with the other.

In other words, stop arguing about price and instead turn to terms. It's positively amazing how often sellers will agree to terms, if you give them their price.

For example, you may be buying a $350,000 property and, after negotiations, your final offer is $317,000. The seller is stuck at $332,000: $15,000 separates you. But you know that your closing costs are going to be roughly $10,000 including points on your loan, title fees, escrow charges, and so on. So why not counter at the seller's last asking price with the contingency that they pay your costs? They'll get their price, something they may be adamant about, and make an extra $5000 over your last offer. You'll get in for no cash (assuming you've worked the financing as indicated in the previous two chapters).

Won't the seller object? Maybe . . . and maybe not. Remember, many sellers are simply hung up on price. Give them their price, in this case sweetened by upping the cash to them by $5000, and they may be happy as clams.

TIP

In a real estate deal, either party can usually pay the other's transaction costs. It all depends on what both parties agree to in the purchase agreement.

The Lender May Not Go Along

Sometimes lenders will not go along with one party paying the closing costs of another. Be sure you have an agreeable lender. If not, you'll have to go looking for one who is more accepting.

Usually lenders will not object to the seller paying your "nonrecurring" closing costs if you're a buyer. These are costs that only occur once, such as title insurance, escrow costs, and some points. They often object to the seller paying your recurring closing costs (such as mortgage interest, fire insurance, and taxes) because it suggests you don't have the wherewithal to really afford the purchase.

Also, if the seller pays some of your buyer's loan points, there's the matter of who gets to deduct or capitalize them for tax purposes. Either party may be able to. Be sure you also first check with your accountant.

Don't think having the other party pay your transaction costs is an unusual occurrence. It happens in deals all the time. However, it will never happen unless you insist upon it. Wise investors make it a regular issue to insist that their closing costs be paid by the other party, even though by doing so they risk losing the deal.

TIP

Sometimes it's better to lose the deal than to have to pay cash for the closing costs. After all, there are millions of homes for sale, but cash is very hard to come by.

Get the Seller to Wrap the Closing Costs into the Loan

You may be able to get the lender to pay all your closing costs (or at least the nonrecurring ones). This is a different way to avoid paying the closing costs from out-of-pocket cash. Here, instead of the seller footing the bill, the lender does. Yes, it can work, but you must be careful to find a lender who is agreeable and doubly careful to be sure the lender is fully aware of what's happening. (You don't want an angry lender to come back later and try either to raise your interest rate or rescind your loan because some vital information was held back.)

To see how this works, let's assume that you're getting a 95 percent loan (putting 5 percent of your own money down). The property is priced at $100,000, so at full price, the loan amount would be $95,000 with you coming up with $5000 down. Further, let's say there's an additional $3000 in closing costs. The question is, how do you finance that $3000?

We'll say that after some negotiations, you and the sellers are agreed on a price of $95,000. (That's a not unreasonable drop of 5 percent off the asking price.)

At this point, and before finally signing off on the last counteroffer, you make this offer to the sellers: Instead of a final purchase price of $95,000, you'll pay the sellers a purchase price of $98,000, $3000 more. And they, in turn, will give you a $3000 credit.

This shouldn't make any difference to the sellers, since they're getting the same money anyhow. However, it will make a big difference to you. At a sales price of $95,000, your mortgage is $90,250. At a $98,000 sales price, the mortgage is now $93,100, or roughly $3000 more. What you've effectively done is create $3000 from the mortgage that will now go to pay your closing costs—you've financed them.

There's no sleight of hand involved. All that's happened is that you're paying a slightly higher price for the property and the sellers, in exchange, are paying your closing costs. It's the same to the sellers— you've just gotten a loan roughly $3000 higher. As I said, you've financed the closing costs.

The Lender May Object

A lender may object to the above transaction. The lender may say that the true sales price was $3000 lower and, thus, so should be the loan.

This makes little sense. The loan is (or should be) based on the value of the property as determined by an honest appraisal. No lender worth its salt will offer a mortgage without an "arm's length" appraisal. And if the property appraises out at the full price (in this case, $98,000), what's the difference how the negotiations went?

In addition, the loan is based on LTV (loan-to-value), not on LTV *plus* closing costs. Thus, so long as you meet the lender's criteria for credit, income, and down payment, you should be entitled to the mortgage.

Nevertheless, if the purchase agreement reflects a price increase at the very end of negotiations, a lender may object by saying that the purpose is to get a higher LTV than is warranted on the property. (In all probability the lender is simply worrying that there's some hanky-panky going on that it isn't aware of and just doesn't want to take any chances.)

You have two ways to avoid this problem. First, find a lender who doesn't object.

Second, make sure your written offer only reflects the final purchase price. You can simply tell the seller what your final offer will be and why you want it handled the way you do. If the seller agrees, write it up that way.

Boost the LTV of the Loan

As we've seen, today if you have good enough credit and your income is sufficiently high, you can get a loan for the entire purchase price of the property. Indeed, in some cases, you can get a loan for 103 percent of the purchase price, meaning the lender will roll your closing costs into the mortgage. In some extreme cases the lender will even go to 125 percent of the purchase price! (If you're not sure about this, reread Chapter 3—and remember, this is usually available only to those who intend to occupy the property.)

TRAP

Beware of getting a 125 percent mortgage. If for any reason you can't make the payments and need to sell quickly, you may find you're "upside-down"—you owe more than your home is worth.

Some lenders offer 125 percent loans. In other words, they will give you 25 percent more than the property's purchase price when you get the mortgage. The problem here is that usually these are not just real estate loans, they are personal loans as well. In other words, you are personally obligated for repayment regardless of what happens to the property. With a real estate mortgage, normally the property is the only thing you lose if you can't make the payments, and it's unlikely (but always possible) that the lender will come after you personally. With a 125 percent mortgage, you're often taking out not only a real estate loan, but a personal loan as well. If the market turns down or you hit hard times and can't make the payments, it's likely the lender will come after you personally if you can't keep up the mortgage payments.

Get the Lender to Wrap the Closing Costs into the Loan

For the buyer, the biggest cash closing costs are usually the points to get the mortgage. If you're getting a mortgage for $300,000 and you've agreed to pay three points, that's $9000 out of your pocket. (One "point" is equal to 1 percent of the mortgage amount. Three points are equal to 3 percent of the mortgage amount.)

In the past there wasn't much you could about this. Today, however, with most lenders you can reduce or even eliminate the points by simply agreeing to pay a slightly higher interest rate. Indeed, the use of points is simply a device that enables the lender to offer you a lower than market rate loan.

It works quite simply. Let's say you're applying for the $300,000 mortgage noted above with $9000 in points. Further, let's say that the interest rate on this mortgage is 6 percent. Now, you make the lender this offer, "Eliminate all of the points, the whole $9000, and charge me a higher interest rate." For instance, instead of 6 percent the rate is now 7 percent.

Will lenders do this? They do it all the time.

TIP

In today's world of real estate financing, exchanging points for a higher interest rate (and the other way round, a lower interest rate for more points) is done routinely.

The lender should be able to make a quick calculation and determine how much higher your interest rate needs to be to offset the points. In our example it was 7 percent, but it could be more or less. Thus by paying a slightly higher interest rate (along with slightly higher monthly payments), you can avoid having to pay cash up front in the form of points.

Keep in mind, however, that now you must qualify for the loan at a higher interest rate. That will usually mean you'll need more income.

Cutting Title Insurance and Escrow Costs

The last of the biggest expenses in the closing costs are the fees that go to the title insurance and escrow companies. In the past, these tended to be relatively small. However, in recent years some companies have jacked up their fees to incredible sizes. Today some companies are charging two and three times what they charged only a decade ago. Therefore, if you could cut these fees, you could save hundreds if not thousands of dollars on a transaction. There are two ways to cut them.

The first is simply to shop around. Title insurance and escrow companies compete for business, and their rates vary in most states. (Some states regulate them.) Check out half a dozen in your area. You'll probably be astonished at the differences. Then, when you're making your deal, insist that the escrow and title insurance be handled through a company with a cheap rate. Once you explain, the other party to the deal should be happy to go along.

TRAP

If you're the seller, the RESPA (Real Estate Settlement Procedure Act) says that you cannot dictate what title insurance company a buyer may use.

Further, agents often want to use a particular title/escrow company. Many agents insist that both buyers and sellers use an escrow and title insurance company affiliated with their real estate company. They often say that this is a title/escrow company they've frequently used in the past and that they feel comfortable that it will handle everything correctly and at minimum cost.

Maybe. But just remember that it's up to you (and the other party) to decide on which escrow and title insurance company to use. The agent can suggest, but cannot normally demand.

TRAP

Bundling of services (where the agent gets a kickback) is unethical, and in some cases illegal, but recommending an affiliated company usually isn't, so long as the affiliation is disclosed and you agree to it.

The second way to reduce the costs is to cut a deal with a particular escrow and title insurance company. After all, remember that you're an investor who's likely to bring in a lot of business. If you're there every six months to a year with another deal, particularly as the properties get more expensive, there's a lot of money to be made for the company.

So tell them that you'll deal with them exclusively. You'll bring all your purchases and sales to them *if* they give you a special rate.

Don't think this is something new or unusual. Title insurance and escrow companies regularly offer reduced rates to better customers. Even if you're just a consumer who happens to sell a house within a year or two after you bought it, the company may cut a deal of anywhere from 5 to 25 percent simply because they have less work to do. If you're an investor who brings in deals on a regular basis, you may be cut a regular discount.

TIP

The reason the title insurance companies say they can offer a reduced "reissue" rate to a consumer who resells a home shortly after buying it is that they don't have to conduct a long search. They only need to search the title back to the purchase, perhaps a few years. Hence, there's less work and less cost. However, many title insurance companies only conduct a search back to the last transaction anyhow, so you have to wonder.

Can you entirely eliminate your transaction costs? Sometimes. But, even if you can't get rid of all of them, with careful planning you should be able to get them greatly reduced.

6

The Big Trap—
Negative Cash Flow

Anybody can buy real estate with little to no cash. We've seen how in the previous chapters. But the real test is not whether you can buy it, but whether you can hold onto it long enough to sell it for a profit (or until your equity grows big enough to refinance your money out).

Buying with little or no cash can lead to problems, as I once observed when riding on a plane to Seattle. I happened to be sitting next to an individual who seemed very nervous—and not about flying. In conversation he revealed that he had taken a course on buying property the "easy way" from a real estate guru. Subsequently, he had gone out and, using only a promissory note (a promise to pay, a personal pledge), he had purchased four separate properties in the Denver area. He had immediately rented them out, only to find that the rental income was just a fraction of the total expenses. He was forced to come up with nearly $2500 a month out of his own pocket just to sustain the four rentals.

Of course, he hoped that price appreciation would allow him to resell quickly for a profit. However, although the market in Denver had been super hot when he had taken his course, it had since cooled down. It looked like he might need a couple of years before he could get out from under. In the meantime, it was breaking his back to come up with the $2500 negative cash flow (the amount of cash he had to put into the properties out of his pocket) each month to keep them solvent. In fact, he had taken an extra job and his wife had also gone to work. Even so, he doubted he could keep it up for more than another couple of months, when the last of his savings would be gone.

I was sympathetic. Instead of buying good investment property, this individual had bought a series of "alligators." (You'll recall that we were first introduced to the concept of alligators in Chapter 1.)

Alligators are properties where the negative cash flow is so high that the property seems to eat you alive, much as a real alligator would. He appreciated my description and wanted to know how to get away from those alligators. I gave him some ideas, but explained that in the process he probably would realize no immediate profits . . . and all the money he had thus far put in could be lost—not a pleasant investment result.

The Curse of Negative Cash Flow

Any property can turn into a negative cash flow alligator. All that's required is for the income to be less than the expenses. The difference doesn't even have to be that much. Just $100 a month in negative cash flow will, after a while, have you pulling your hair out. Yes, you may be able to afford it. But it will taint your investment experience, and eventually you'll rue the day you bought that property.

Positive cash flow properties are what we all want. Even if that positive cash flow is only $100 a month, we can point to it and say with pride, "I'm making money!" With negative cash flow, the opposite is true. Every month we'll look at that property and say, "It's losing me money!"

Yes, it may all come out in the wash at the end if eventually you're able to sell for a profit. However, waiting for that happy result can make your life miserable. And it can cause you to sell prematurely, sometimes at a loss, just to get out from under.

The Link between Alligators and Little-to-No-Cash Investors

As I said, any property can become an alligator. The rental market can turn sour. The house may need unexpected and costly repairs. The neighborhood may go bad.

TRAP

The biggest single reason that most people find themselves wed to a financial alligator is that they put little
to no cash into a bad property. It's the single likeliest
cause of negative cash flow.

Look at it this way: The more money you put into a home, the
smaller your mortgage(s) will be. The smaller the mortgage LTV, the
lower the interest rate is likely to be. And the smaller the mortgage
and the lower the interest rate, the lower the monthly payments.

On the other hand, the less money you put in, the bigger the
mortgage is likely to be. And, of course, the higher the LTV, as we
saw in Chapter 3, the higher the interest rate. All of which leads to
higher monthly payments.

Thus the conundrum: Yes, you can get into a property for little to
no cash, but you must be careful of the property you choose. If getting in means buying an alligator, the best investment choice you
can make may be to stay away.

This is not to say, of course, that every little-to-no-cash property is
an alligator. If you buy right, you won't have a problem. In the next
chapter, we're going to discuss how to find those properties that will
not bite you. For the remainder of this chapter, we're going to discuss what it means to have a good property versus an alligator.

Calculate Your Cash Flow before You Buy

The key to avoiding the purchase of an alligator is to know what goes
into cash flow. Think of it as a ledger. On one side is income, on the
other side are expenses. You want both sides to at least balance. If
there's more income, then you'll have positive cash flow and be a
happy camper. If there are more expenses, you're not going to be
very happy at all.

It's easy to keep track of income from a rental property; it's usually one check (or cash) paid to you. It's more difficult to track
expenses since there are both recurring costs that occur each month
(such as mortgage payments) and variable costs that occur only
occasionally.

Typical Recurring Expenses on a Rental

- Mortgage payment (interest, principal, and taxes/insurance, if included in the loan)
- Water (and any other utility bill)
- Gardener, pool service, any other monthly service
- Home owner's fee
- Taxes (if paid separately)
- Insurance (if paid separately)
- Regular maintenance

Typical Occasional Expenses on a Rental

- Repair—cost of materials and workers
- Vacancies (between tenants)
- Clean-up (when a tenant moves out to prepare for a new tenant)
- Advertising (to find a new tenant)
- Special—unanticipated expenses

Before you buy you should try to determine, as accurately as possible, most of your expenses, such as the mortgage payment, taxes, and insurance. Some of your other costs, such as maintenance, gardener or pool service, and even home owner's fees, may be harder to define as these can increase suddenly. And your occasional costs will be even harder to get a handle on.

Nevertheless, you should make a best guess estimate of what these will cost you. You should do this on both an annual and a monthly basis, even though some expenses only occur once or twice a year.

TIP

I find an annual income/expenses estimate to be more helpful when evaluating a purchase. On the other hand, a monthly income/expense evaluation is a necessity once you own the property and are a landlord.

Thus, you'll end up with an income/expense estimate that should look something like this:

Annual Income/Expense Estimate for 29 Magnolia Lane

Annual Income (from Anticipated Rents)	$18,000
Annual Expenses	

Mortgage payment (including interest, principal, and taxes/insurance)	$15,000
Water	600
Gardener, pool service, any other monthly service	0
Home owner's fee (it's a single-family home)	0
Taxes	(paid in mortgage pmt.)
Insurance	(paid in mortgage pmt.)
Regular maintenance	600
Repair	600
Vacancies (1 month's rent)	1500
Clean-up (when tenant moves out to prepare for new tenant)	500
Advertising (to find new tenant)	100
Special—unanticipated expenses	900
	$19,800

As you can see, the annual income from 29 Magnolia Lane is anticipated to be $18,000 a year. However, the annual expenses are anticipated to be $19,800 a year. Now, do we have a good property, or are we talking alligator here?

This property will cost you $1800 a year out of pocket to maintain, assuming that your estimates are correct. Of course, that's paid monthly, so it will cost you an average of $150 a month out of pocket.

Can you afford $150 a month, every month? Do you have enough monthly income from other sources to cover this negative cash flow? Or will it nag at you, as suggested earlier, until it becomes such a headache that you'll sell at any price?

If you have the financial and emotional resources to handle this amount of negative flow, then, although this property is an alligator, it's a very small one, and you may be willing and able to take its bite every month. You're willing to do this if and only if you can see light at the end of the tunnel—that is, if you can see a profit down the road.

How do you know if the property will be profitable?

Do the Long-Term Profits Warrant the Short-Term Cost?

Now you have to conduct a different kind of analysis. Since real estate is generally a long-term investment (except for flipping, described in Chapter 8), you'll have to estimate what your profits will be after a period of time. I arbitrarily pick five to seven years. Of course, you may hold the property longer, but I personally think this is a reasonable time for a property to turn a profit. If it hasn't by then, you may have a real stinker on your hands.

The key here is to try to figure out what price appreciation will do over the next five years at minimum. Will it go up by 5 percent? Or 10 percent? Or will it be a negative figure that actually goes down?

Of course, no one can know for sure. But there are some sources that can be helpful in determining price appreciation or depreciation in your area.

Sources for Predicting Price Appreciation

- Check with your local Real Estate Board through an agent for the 30 year price history of your area. Many Boards maintain these. While the past is no guarantee of the future, if prices in your area have appreciated, say, 4 percent a year over the last 30 years, it's at least a good indication they might continue to do so over the next 5.

- Check with HUD (the Department of Housing and Urban Development). It maintains records of price appreciation going back at least 30 years. The Web site is *www.hud.org*.

- Check with private services that do prognostications such as found on *www.dataquick.com*. These often charge a fee, but they will sometimes give you five-year estimates.

- Check with a few real estate brokers in your area. See what they are quoting as the typical price appreciation to expect. Keep in mind, however, that brokers are in the business of selling property and their estimates may be tilted a bit toward the optimistic side.

Let's say that you figure prices are going to rise 5 percent a year over the next five years. If you buy a property that costs $250,000, here's what the price appreciation will look like.

Price Appreciation at 5 Percent Annually on a $250,000 Property

Length of Time Held	Appreciated Value
Year 1	262,000
Year 2	273,100
Year 3	286,755
Year 4	301,093
Year 5	336,147

After five years, you would expect your $250,000 to be worth roughly $336,000. If we take 10 percent or $33,600 off that for transaction costs (assuming you use an agent and don't sell the property yourself), you end up with a profit of roughly $50,000. Sound good?

On the other hand, you've been taking $150 a month or $1800 a year out of your pocket to keep the place going. After five years you've paid $9000, reducing your profits to slightly more than $40,000. (Of course, during that five years you might expect rental income to rise, thus reducing your negative cash flow and increasing your profit.)

Is it worthwhile to make $40,000 plus on a little-to-no-cash investment over five years? I'll let you answer that question for yourself.

Keep in mind, of course, that other factors that we have mentioned could also have an effect (lower or higher appreciation, higher or lower vacancies, fewer or greater repairs and maintenance, and so on).

The big key to all this, as you may have surmised, is buying a property for a low enough price to avoid any negative cash flow altogether or buying it for a low enough price that you can afford to absorb the negative cash flow for a number of years. How do you make that calculation?

The 1 Percent Rule

You can go through the income expense procedure just outlined. However, I've found one rule-of-thumb that works amazingly well.

It's called the 1 percent rule, and it works in low-interest-rate markets, like the one we've recently experienced. (The old rule was 2 percent, but that applied when mortgage rates were around 8 to 10 percent annually.)

The rule simply says that you figure out what 1 percent of your mortgage is, and that should equal one month's rental income. If it's more than one month's rental income, you're paying too much for the property from a negative-cash-flow perspective.

Let's take an example. You buy a property for $100,000 with no cash down so that you can have a mortgage for the full amount. If you can rent that property for 1 percent of the mortgage, or $1000 a month, you should have a positive cash flow. Does it work?

Monthly Expenses (Estimated) on a $100,000 Property

Mortgage payment (@ 6 percent)	$550
Water	40
Gardener, pool service, any other monthly service	0
Home owner's fee (it's a single-family home)	0
Taxes	125
Insurance	50
Regular maintenance and repair	50
Vacancies (1 month's rent)	90
Advertising (to find new tenant)	10
Special—unanticipated—expenses	35
	$950

You should have around $50 positive cash flow. Of course, it all depends on what you calculate for expenses.

Does it work every time? Nope, it doesn't. But I've found it to work a lot of the time. However, if I'm serious about the property, I'll still need to do my homework and create a full income/expense sheet to be sure. Now all that's required is to find a property where the 1 percent rule applies.

This isn't always an easy proposition, but we'll see how in the next few chapters. In the meantime, another way to go to avoid negative cash flow problems is to cut expenses.

Can expenses really be cut? Sometimes, but you need to adopt a creative attitude. (By they way, this is also an excellent exercise after you've bought a property and find that you bought poorly and expenses are eating you up.)

Cutting Expenses to Reduce Negative Cash Flow

Mortgage

Since this is a fixed expense, the only realistic way to cut it is to refinance to a lower interest rate or a different type of mortgage. A lower interest rate will produce a lower monthly payment. Moving from a fixed rate mortgage to an adjustable rate one could also produce a lower monthly payment, at least for a few years. (This means that you will need to sell or refinance again after a few years if the adjustable's rate and monthly payments go up.)

Taxes

The only way to lower this amount is to have the property's tax value reassessed. But this is unlikely to produce a reduction unless property values overall have been dropping. (Indeed, a reassessment in a hot market can actually result in an increase in taxes!)

Insurance

It might be possible to produce a marginal reduction in costs by seeking out a cheaper insurance policy.

Water

The temptation is to make the tenants pay for water (as they do for other utilities) and cut this cost. That, however, would be a mistake. The result could be that the tenants cut back on watering the landscaping, which would then die and adversely affect the overall value of the property.

Gardener

Again, ridding yourself of the gardener could be a mistake. If you need a gardener, then it's best to keep one. Don't be deluded into thinking that tenants will be thrilled to do heavy landscaping maintenance for a property they are only renting. An alternative is for the investor/owner to spend a few days a month doing the gardening.

Maintenance

This can be a heavy expense. If you call a plumber out to fix a washer, you may incur a $100 charge for a 25-cent part. Most investors cut these costs to the bare minimum by doing the work themselves.

Repairs

Are you lucky? Is your house old or new? Newer homes tend to have far fewer repairs (which is an incentive for buying newer properties). In any property you might go several years with no expenses for repair at all. Then in one year you might need to replace or repair a water heater, a furnace/air conditioner, and a suddenly leaking roof. It could cost you $5000 to $10,000 or more in repairs. This category of expenses is always an uncertainty. As I said, "Are you lucky?"

TRAP

You can't put off repairs in a rental the way you might be able to in your own house. You might tolerate a broken window for a few weeks. But it's a liability issue with tenants, who won't tolerate cold/hot air coming in. Their perspective is that they are paying rent (sometimes a very high rent), and their expectations are that the premises will be habitable and at least in as good a condition as when they originally rented. It's up to you to make it so.

Special

Who knows? Again, it's a matter of luck.

Increase the Income

Can you increase rents to cover expenses?

It's unlikely. You can do some things to make the property more valuable to renters. You can paint and recarpet, even offer to throw in a gardener. Doing all this may make a little difference, but like property values, rental values are what they are. Tenants are not fools. If you're asking $1000 a month and they can rent a similar property across the street for $900, which one do you think they'll rent?

TRAP

Overall, rentals go pretty much for their rental market value. And that's mainly determined by their location, size, and—mostly—by the number of tenants with the ability to pay in your area.

All of which is to say that, barring a big change in the rental market upward (or downward!), you're pretty much going be stuck with your original rental income. Of course, be sure that you're charging as much as the unit warrants. Don't charge less. But don't hold out hopes of charging more.

Don't Overlook Those Tax Savings

Some investors feel that they can easily afford to sustain a cash loss on their rental property because they'll make it up in tax savings at the end of the year. This may or may not be a reasonable assumption.

There are rules that can limit losses on real estate that can be applied to your ordinary income. We'll go into taxes on investment rentals in more detail in Chapter 12. But for now, let's just say that unless your personal income is under $100,000 a year, you may not be able to deduct all of your negative cash flow from your rental property (either in cash or from depreciation) each year. If your personal income is over $150,000, you may not be able to deduct any losses from rental income in the year incurred!

Be sure you're clear on what we mean by losses against personal income. If allowed, you can only take the loss on your rental property as a *deduction* against your other ordinary income. You cannot take it as a *credit.* What's the difference? A deduction lowers the income on which you pay taxes. For example, if your taxable income is $100,000 and you have a rental loss of $15,000, your taxable income is reduced to $85,000.

A credit, on the other hand, is a reduction of your taxes. If you owe $15,000 in taxes and you have a $15,000 tax credit, your taxes are reduced to $0.

Losses on rental property, when allowed, are a deduction, not a credit. They reduce your income and, depending on your tax bracket, result in some tax savings. They do not directly reduce the taxes you owe.

Finally, remember income must be offset by rental expenses before determining whether you made or lost money. You may think this is a ridiculous mistake, but a surprisingly large percentage of newcomers to real estate investing make it. First you determine your total rental income, then your total expenses for the rental. If your total expenses exceed your total income, then you have a loss, which may or may not be deducted from your personal income.

Get Good Tax Advice

Even if you've never used an accountant before, when you first buy rental property you should get a good accountant to look over your tax situation. Your accountant should be able to tell you quite accurately what tax savings, if any, you'll get from owning the property. (The accountant can also prepare the depreciation schedule for your property—something that can be tricky to do.) If you have an allowable deduction, then you can apply it against your monthly personal negative cash flow to reduce it.

7
Finding Good Rentals

It's unfortunate, but when no one wants real estate and the market is stone cold, you can easily find all sorts of great investment bargains. On the other hand, when everyone wants to buy and there's a hot market like we've seen in recent years, it's difficult to find good investment properties.

But it's not impossible.

It's kind of like playing poker. In poker a big key to the game is patience. You might have to throw in 30 hands before you get a good one that you're willing to play. Finding a good real estate investment property is similar. You might have to investigate 30 properties and reject them before you find the right one.

In this chapter we're going to see what makes for a good rental—a worthwhile property to purchase for investment. We're talking about locating properties and analyzing them in terms of how high and how reliable their rental income will be. Also, how much they are going to cost us over and above fixed costs such as mortgage, taxes, and insurance.

What about High-Priced Areas?

Before getting started, a few words about finding good investment properties in high-priced areas such as many parts of the East and West coasts and in major cities. Although the median price of a home nationwide may still be around $200,000, the price for an entry level investment home in these areas may be closer to $300,000, $400,000, and much higher.

At these higher prices, it's often hard to find a home that you can rent out for even a small negative cash flow, let alone a breakeven. In fact, at my Web site (*www.robertirwin.com*), probably the most common question I get is how to find good rentals in high-priced areas.

I have two answers. The first is, "Dig harder." For example, I have some friends who live in a Los Angeles neighborhood where the homes average around $700,000 apiece (not unusually high for good areas in LA). They are looking for a good rental property. Recently they noticed that a home across the street from theirs was for sale. When they called to find the price, they were told it was $250,000. Naturally they went to see it, but it was a disaster inside, a real fixer-upper. While they were debating whether or not to make an offer, it sold—for full price.

A few months later the same house was back on the market. This time the price was $450,000. The original buyer had made a number of cosmetic improvements, however it still looked fairly bad. My friends began making a list of things they would need to do and the costs and, of course, the house was sold out from under them again.

Currently, it's back on the market for $650,000 and has been for sitting for a while. The current owners still have not made all the necessary improvements, and buyers are hesitant to pay top dollar price for a home that remains in run-down condition. But as a rental . . . ?

The moral?

Good properties are everywhere. They are likely to be in your neighborhood, if not right now, sometime in the not-too-distant future. The key is to recognize them and to act quickly. If my friends had bought when the house was first offered, or even on the second go around, they could have acquired an excellent rental property, after some fix-up. (They confirmed this too late, with an income/expenses analysis sheet.)

The second alternative is to look in lower priced areas. Every major city has higher priced as well as lower priced areas. Often the lower priced areas are excellent areas for finding good rental homes. Frequently these are nearer the city center, or further out. (The distance from cultural and financial hubs often makes the big difference.)

I'm not suggesting that you buy in a slum area. But you may want to consider looking in a less costly area where price-to-rental income may be more favorable.

TRAP

Beware of buying rental real estate at a distance from your home.

Properties don't require constant care. But they do require your attention for getting them rented, for fixing big and small things that go wrong, for answering tenants' questions, and on and on. You'll find that the closer you are to your rental (assuming you're not right next door, which can present other problems from tenants who are overly friendly), the easier it is to deal with these problems.

That's not to say you can't handle them at a distance. You can hire a property management firm. However, they typically charge 8 to 12 percent of your monthly income for their services, and they tend to bill out all maintenance or repairs at high rates. Few starting investors can afford this.

Or, you can make an arrangement with a tenant to handle most problems on their own for a reduced rent. I've successfully done this many times. In fact, one tenant of mine found a broken water pipe in the house. He bought a soldering gun, some copper pipe and solder, and fixed it on his own, charging me only for the materials. As I said, you can sometimes get such good arrangements. But you can't count on it.

Therefore, to play it safe you should try to buy close to home. Or, and this is admittedly a major change, consider moving to an area where prices are lower and rental home opportunities are more plentiful.

Move?

I'm sure some readers are astounded that I would suggest this. But they shouldn't be. Remember, we're talking about a financial plan that lasts upward of 20 years and allows you to retire wealthy. Perhaps moving to another area for a few years isn't such a big sacrifice to make. Besides, if you're going for that great financing mentioned in Chapter 3, you're going to need to move in anyhow. Maybe now is the time to make that big change and get started on the road to real estate wealth.

Finding a Good Rental Area

A good rental area is where tenants are plentiful and can afford the rents you want to charge and there isn't an oversupply of rental housing. How do you find such an area? There are many clues.

To begin, look for an area where there are many employers to provide a steady base of employed tenants. Typically this is an area where there are lots of industries providing jobs.

However, you want to be sure that your rental matches the types of jobs available. For example, if there's a manufacturing plant in town that provides a lot of stable blue-collar workers who can afford to pay up to $1300 a month in rent, a property that you can rent for under $1300 a month (and still pay your expenses) would be a sound investment.

On the other hand, a property that requires you to bring in $2000 a month would make little sense in this area. You'd have nothing but long periods of vacancy.

Perhaps in another community there's an industrial park that provides lots of high-paying white-collar workers who can easily afford to make those $2500 a month payments. Now your home with the $2000 plus rental makes good sense. However, in this community you might actually have trouble renting out a home for only $1300—it might be too small or lack features that the tenant population demands.

TRAP

Your rental property must suit your rental market.

But how do you find out what the rental market around you is like? One way is to do a thorough investigation. Check with the local

Chamber of Commerce for the types of employers in the area. Then call on a number of them to find out what kind of tenants they are likely to offer.

Or, you can call a few real estate agents in the area who specialize in property management and just ask. In a few sentences they should be able to tell you what the market is like. Further, if you have a particular house (or other property) in mind, they should be able to give you a fairly accurate estimate of just how much you can rent it for. This is particularly the case if they are farming the area (know it very well).

Can you rely on such word-of-mouth opinions? I have. But confirm these reports by checking the local newspaper rental section. These are always divided up by area. Find the area your subject home is in and call a few landlords. Find out what they're offering and how much they're charging. You should be able to get a conclusive answer within three or four calls. Also, when you check the paper, look at the quantity of rental ads. A huge amount of ads suggests that perhaps there are too many rentals (or not enough tenants) in your area.

After you've determined that the market is good for rentals, do an analysis of the home. Note: This must be accurate but does not have to take a long time to do. The time invested shouldn't be so long that doing the analysis causes you to lose out on a good deal.

Look for a property that will pretty much run itself—one that won't require constant maintenance and repair. Here are some general rules.

Rules to Observe When Looking for a Good Rental

- **Avoid older homes**. They tend to need more care.
- **Avoid large lots** (and corner lots, which also tend to be large). You'll end up spending too much money on water and gardening.
- **Avoid homes with pools** (unless you're in an expensive area where pools are the rule). Finding good pool maintenance people who don't charge an arm and a leg can be difficult.
- **Avoid large homes**. You'll find you'll end up renting to large families with lots of kids, and the kids tend to put more wear and tear on the house than adults.

- **Be careful of buying homes very close to a detracting neighborhood anchor,** such as a mall, gas station, factory, freeway on-ramp, and so on. These homes often sell for less, and they do make good rentals; but they may not appreciate as fast, and you may not get as much when you sell.
- **Be careful of homes on busy streets.** Again, this knocks down their price, which can make them better choices as rentals, but they can be difficult to resell later on.

These are the guidelines, but as we know, few people actually follow guidelines. So let's look at the problems you're likely to run into if you don't follow some of the rules just noted.

Avoid Older Homes

Here's a list of problems that you, and your tenants, are likely to run into in older homes:

- **Plumbing distress**—From leaking faucets (which you have to run out and fix) to leaking pipes (which require moving the tenant out while the house is replumbed).

- **Electrical distress**—From light switches and plugs that suddenly burn out to overloaded circuits which, if not fixed, can threaten fire. Older homes tend to have wiring that's too lightweight for today's modern appliances. Tenants can easily overload it by plugging too many heaters, lights, washers, or other appliances into the same circuit, blowing fuses and circuit breakers. This can necessitate expensive rewiring.

- **Roof leaks**—You might put up with a bucket for a while, but a tenant will want it fixed instantly.

- **Worn-out appliances**—You might keep them running for a few years by tenderly caring for them. Tenants will simply turn them on full and, if they don't work, expect instant replacements.

- **System problems**—From termites in the floor to bad heaters and air conditioning. If you're in the place, you can tolerate it a while, perhaps even do some of the repair or replacement work yourself. If you have a tenant, it will have to be done immediately or you'll lose the tenant—and your rent.

A new house, preferably one less than 25 years old and, ideally, less than 10 years old, will largely avoid such problems. Newer properties have newer plumbing, electrical, roofs, appliances, and systems. There's far less chance of anything expensive going out.

Avoid Bigger Homes

The problem is that the more people that occupy the property, the more wear and tear (and potentially damage) to it there is. This goes double for children, who in their play tend to bump, dent, gouge, and even chew up walls, floors, doors, and so forth.

The old adage of landlords used to be, "I love children, in your place not mine!" However, antidiscrimination laws prohibit you from refusing to rent to a family because it has children. You can, though, refuse to rent if the home is too small to accommodate a large family. Therein lies the reason for not having too many bedrooms.

Although I've never found a hard and fast rule that says how many people, at maximum, can occupy a bedroom (some fire regulations put it at four!), it's a cinch that the more bedrooms you have, the more people can reasonably occupy the property. It stands to reason that a house with four to six bedrooms can have more people in it than a house with only one, even if both properties have the same square footage.

Does that mean that a one-bedroom house makes a good rental? Not usually. You won't find many tenants (or many buyers, subsequently) that want only one bedroom. But two- and three-bedroom properties do make good rentals—while four- and five-bedroom properties usually do not.

Avoid Big Lots

If you're the sort of person who likes room to roam, buy yourself a house with a big lot to live in. But, if you're an investor, avoid them like the plague.

A big lot requires big maintenance. If it's got lots of lawn and landscaping, you'll need to hire (and pay for) a gardener to take care of it. You can't count on the tenants to do that; after all, it's not their yard.

The bigger the lot, the more upkeep is involved. Yet, when it comes time to resell, you'll find that a big lot will only marginally return you any more money. In some markets, it may actually get a reduced price!

As noted earlier, always pay the water bill yourself. (Have the tenants pay the other utilities). The only way you can be sure that your landscaping will be watered is if you're paying for it. If the tenants pay the water bill, they may refuse to water the landscaping to cut costs. (After all, it's not their lawn, trees, and bushes that are suffering.)

Avoid Pool Homes

There are two reasons: upkeep and liability. Until you have a pool, you can't believe how much upkeep is required to be sure it's clean and swimmable. Let a pool go, and you'll find that algae very quickly destroys the plaster and filters, that equipment deteriorates, and that bringing it back up to par, if possible, can be very costly.

A pool is also a big liability headache. Of course, there's always the chance that someone could fall in and drown. To protect yourself you'll need at least a 5-foot fence with a self-closing gate all the way around the pool. And you'll need to rely on your tenants to maintain the fence and gate. Finally, the insurance to protect yourself when you own a pool home can be very costly.

In addition, even if the pool is protected, unless the water is properly filtered and cleaned, there's always the danger that a swimmer could get sick from swimming in it. You can be sure that if this happens and there's a lawsuit, you will as owner/investor be named. As I said, if you buy a rental with a pool, you'll want to carry a big liability insurance policy. The bigger the better, but I would never get one for less than $2 million.

Always hire a pool service to maintain the pool. Don't rely on tenants to do this. Even if they want to, they often forget or do something incorrect that ends up costing you even more money.

Be Careful with Condos and Co-Ops

We've talked about buying a condo or a co-op as a rental because the initial investment is usually lower than for a house. Many people do successfully rent condos for years. Recently, in many areas, their price appreciation has been higher than for single-family homes.

However, you have to be careful with a condo and especially careful with a co-op. The reason is the HOA (home owner's association) or the Board (of Directors). All condos are part of a HOA, including any you'll buy. And the HOA will set the rules for everything from changes you can make to the exterior to noise in the evening to where cars can be parked. Boards set similar rules for co-ops.

In other words, there are lots of rules. Hence, when renting a condo or co-op expect all sorts of initial problems during the rent-up period (such as restrictions on putting up a "For Rent" sign"— although recent laws in some states have eliminated this problem).

Further, expect continuing problems with the HOA or Board. Although owners tend to follow the rules, if reluctantly, because they realize rules are there to keep up the overall value of the property, tenants have fewer constraints. Tenants could care less about property values, since they don't own the property. Expect your neighbor owners to complain at the drop of a hat about your tenants' activities. And expect to be fined and chastised by the HOA or Board over what your tenants do. There's often a lot of hassle that you'll have to put up with.

Of course, as I say, it can be well worth it in the end if you get rapid price appreciation and can refinance, cash out, or sell for a big profit.

Is the Property Ready to Be Rented?

A clean home will usually rent quickly to a clean tenant. But to sell a home, it will have to be more than just clean. It will have to look new.

TRAP

If you fix up a property to rent, you only need to go so far. You don't have to remodel it.

However, if you fix up a property to sell, you need to go much further. You may need to paint everywhere, recarpet, replace appliances, cabinets, countertops, and so forth.

Therefore, when buying a property that you plan to rent out, you don't have to look for a property that's been upgraded and is spotless. It only needs to be serviceable and clean. And this should be reflected in a more reasonable price.

On the other hand, if the property you're considering has been fixed up to sell, chances are the seller has spent a great deal of time, money, and effort on it. And this also will be reflected, but in a higher price.

As an investor looking to rent out a home, you don't really care about that extra effort made to bring the home up to selling condition. You're more interested in a lower price.

Therefore, don't pay for a Cadillac when you only need a Chevy. Don't buy a home for a rental that's been primped for sale. You're throwing your money away.

Keep in mind that you can always rent a thoroughly fixed-up home to tenants. However, the chances are that those tenants over the course of a few years will bring that home down to rental condition. By the time you're ready to resell years later, the home may still need a complete reconditioning.

What about the Neighborhood?

You must buy in a sound neighborhood, one that will remain solid year after year. But, you can never guarantee a neighborhood. They change over time. Sometimes, not always, today's blue-collar or white-collar neighborhood will become tomorrow's slum. If you buy into a neighborhood that turns sour, you'll own a home in an area where you may eventually be afraid to go and collect the rent!

But how do you identify a good long-lasting neighborhood?

Quite frankly, short of having a crystal ball, no one can know for sure what will happen to a neighborhood 25 years down the road. However, some things tend to remain constant. If the neighborhood is near good schools and shopping and "looks good" with lots of trees and landscaping; if it's away from industry, commercial settings, and heavily trafficked streets; and, most important, if it's recognized as a "good neighborhood" when you buy, then chances are it will remain so for a long time to come.

When you're buying for the short term, you can ignore a neighborhood problem such as a large commercial center or run-down homes a few streets over. But you can't ignore such things when you buy for the long term.

What's the Local Economy Like?

When buying a property for investment, you'd be in error not to take into consideration the local economy. You could do everything else right and still be tripped up by a market that's turning bad. Put simply, when the economy is booming, lots of people have jobs and can afford to rent. In a local booming economy, you should do well buying a rental property.

Also, check the supply of housing. Some areas of the country, such as the Northeast, have long had an oversupply of housing and a limited demand, though that has turned around in recent years, particularly in popular areas such as around Boston. Other parts of the country, notably the Southwest and in particular the southern part of California, have long had housing shortages and a high demand.

TRAP

As of this writing, the demand for housing in southern California and other parts of the country is far outstripping the supply, pushing rental and housing prices to all-time highs!

There are many sources for determining the health of the local economy and the housing supply. You can check the business section of the local newspaper which, after a week or two of reading, should give you a good overall picture. Also check with the local Chamber of Commerce (although you should expect a positive tone on even a negative situation).

The Department of Labor and the Department of Commerce can provide statistics on employment and growth in your area (at Web sites *www.dol.gov* and *www.doc.gov*). A visit to the local county planning department can tell you how much new development is coming. Your local real estate agent can be a source for an overall perspective.

And when all else fails, check the "fast food index." Are there lots of new fast food chains opening in the area? The people who run these spend millions determining where the best growth areas are. You can reap the benefit of their investigations by following their lead. (Be careful of an area where fast food chains are dying out—it bodes ill for the local economy.)

The Bottom Line

We've looked over some of the parameters you will want to check into when buying a rental property. The big four to keep in mind are the following.

- The supply of tenants (the rental market)
- The type of housing available locally
- The condition of the property
- The local economy and housing supply

Pay attention to these and you shouldn't go far astray in finding a good rental.

8

Flip Quickly or Hold Long Term?

The superheated market of the last few years has spawned a whole new type of investor, one whose goal is not to own real estate long term, but to churn it. (*Churn* in this sense means turning it over quickly to get profits out.) The term used to describe this technique in real estate is *flipping*.

An investor who flips property sometimes does not even take title. Instead, he or she gains control of the property from a seller and then quickly sells the property to a buyer. The investor is actually a middleman who reaps a profit from the difference between a lower buying price and a higher selling price.

Sometimes the profits are huge—$50,000 or more on a house. Sometimes they are small—amounting to only a few thousand dollars. Either way, the goal of the flip investor is to continue churning, making money every time there's a transaction while never really holding on to the real estate.

What should be obvious is that flipping works best in a superheated market where sellers don't fully grasp how quickly prices are going up. In this market an investor can step in and "freeze" a price from a seller and then, because the market is moving up so rapidly, resell for a higher price to a buyer. Flipping does not work very well in a normal or a cold market where prices are more stable or are dropping.

There's nothing wrong with flipping properties, so long as it's done correctly. Indeed, any time you can quickly resell for a cash profit, you probably should do so. The reason is that it's relatively hard to get cash out of real estate. (Remember, it's basically an illiq-uid investment.)

The vast majority of the time, however, you won't be able to flip a property but will instead need to hold it for the long term. Therefore, my advice is to look at every property long term. However, if a flippable property suddenly jumps up in front of you, by all means take advantage of it.

In this chapter we're going to learn how you can flip properties as well as when to hold on to them.

The Rules for Flipping

Rules for Flipping

---

1. **Buy right**—You can only flip if you buy below market price.
2. **Lock in a price**—If the seller can get out of the deal, he or she may try to get the higher resale price themselves.
3. **Have a buyer waiting in the wings**—These are fast deals, you don't have time to go looking for a buyer.
4. **Provide full disclosure**—The way to avoid trouble in these deals is to make sure everyone knows everything. (We'll have more to say about this shortly.)

Getting Started

Have you ever seen lines of people waiting outside the sales office when new homes go up for sale?

This happens when the market is hot and there are shortages of homes. Do you think that all of those people are waiting in line to buy a home to live in? If you do, you would be mistaken. (Note: In many parts of the country there has been a severe housing shortage for at least the last 10 years.)

Many of those people are hoping to flip the property. If there are 20 new homes being built and the demand is for 100 (as has been the case in some areas over recent years), that means that 80 people are not going to get a new home. If you're one of the lucky 20, you can quickly sell to one of the unlucky others.

In a hot market, flipping also takes place in resales. Savvy investors locate properties that are for sale at below market, tie them up, and then quickly resell. Sometimes the sales are from foreclosures, or REOs (real estate owned by banks), or probates, or just from sellers who want out quickly and are willing to take less.

On the other hand, when the market slows down, there's little to flip. It's much easier to find bargain properties (those selling below market), but it's much harder to find buyers who are willing to move quickly. The reason is that when the market slows down, buyers become more cautious. They want to see that they are getting a bargain. Therefore, in order to flip, you have to reduce your profit and give the buyer a good reason to purchase quickly.

TIP

To flip you usually must buy a property *below* market value and resell it at market value.

If you buy at or only slightly below market, you will have to hold on to the property until it goes up before you can resell. (Remember, there are transaction costs so buying slightly below market won't help much unless prices are accelerating rapidly.)

TRAP

Beware of trying to sell for more than market value. Except when the market's red hot and there are multiple offers on every property, you're unlikely to succeed.

The Mechanics of Flipping a Property

The mechanics of the deal are fairly straightforward. Once you locate a property that's below market, you present your offer. If the seller accepts, you have a period of time in which to resell. Depending on how that offer was structured, your time period can be anywhere from a minimum of about 30 days to a maximum of about 6 months. After that, the property is usually considered a keeper, one that you will hold long term. However, if you buy, take title, and hold a property, there's no reason you can't resell it in, say, 8 months, or a year, or 18 months. Some call this flipping, too.

You then bring in a rebuyer (the one who actually purchases the property) who concludes the sale with the original seller. The cash transfer is done in escrow. The new buyer gets a mortgage and puts up a cash down payment in the usual fashion. A portion of the purchase price goes to cash out the original seller. And you get the remainder, usually in cash, but sometimes in the form of a second mortgage for yourself.

Freezing the Seller's Price— the Option

There are two usual methods of flipping, assignment and options. The one I prefer is the option. A real estate option is quite straightforward. Real estate options are, in reality, not much different from stock options. For the buyer, they are an opportunity (but not a requirement) to purchase for a set price by some future date. For the seller, they are a commitment to sell for a set price by a set date. Here's how they work.

You locate the property and make an option offer. If the seller accepts, you give the seller some option money. He or she gives you the option to buy the property at a fixed price for a certain amount of time. You now have a period of time, typically six months, in which the property is tied up.

During the option time, you find a rebuyer. Then you exercise your option by buying the property, or in our case, by selling your option to a rebuyer for a profit. (The process is all handled through escrow.) Note that in an option, you, the buyer, are *not* committed to purchase. It's at your discretion. The seller, however, is committed to sell. He or she must go through with the transaction *if* you execute your option.

Why would a seller agree to such a thing? Cash!

As noted, in order to get an option, you pay the seller some money. It can be any amount, but it has to be enough to persuade him or her to give you an option. A typical amount might be between $500 and $5000, depending on the value of the property.

The term of the option is likewise negotiable. Usually they run from 30 days to 6 months, but they can be longer . . . or shorter.

Let's look at an example. You find a property that is $25,000 below market. Instead of buying it, you give the seller $1500 for an option to buy the property at full *asking* price ($25,000 below market) anytime during the next three months. Now, you've locked in the price and the property.

Next, you find a buyer for the property at full *market* price. You have about two months (plus a month to close) to accomplish this. Once you find your buyer, you "sell" that person the property (actually, your option to buy). Escrow is opened and as part of the process, your option is exercised.

The rebuyer purchases the property, technically by exercising the option. As a practical matter, the rebuyer gets a new mortgage and puts up a down payment; the seller gets his or her price as defined by the option agreement; and you get the difference, in the case of our example, $25,000.

Option Advantages

- You tie up the property at a fixed price.
- You don't need much cash.
- You don't have to qualify for or obtain a mortgage. You also don't have to come up with a down payment. And since you don't own the property, you're not responsible for mortgage payments, taxes, insurance, maintenance, or repairs
- You have time to find a buyer, as long as six months or more.

Option Disadvantages

- You have to put up some money, which is gone whether or not you make the purchase. (If you make the purchase, the money may or may not be applied to the purchase price, depending on how the option is written.)
- You have a limited amount of time to act before your option expires.
- If property values go down during the option period, you'll have trouble finding a buyer.

I've given and taken options on real estate. They can work for both buyers and sellers. For a buyer, we've seen some obvious advantages such as tying up the property for a small amount of money and providing time to locate a rebuyer and conclude a sale. For a seller, they provide either income (the option money) or a sale.

When the Seller Doesn't Want to Give You an Option

The biggest problem with options, as far as I'm concerned, is that most sellers want a quick sale—not a delayed one. They may be facing foreclosure or other financial problems. There could be a divorce or a death in the family. Or, they may simply want to get out so they can move to another home and get on with their lives.

In all such cases, they may need to get cash immediately. Your offer of an option may be appealing, but it won't cut the mustard if they need to be out of the property within 30 days (which, indeed, may be the compelling reason they are willing to sell for a low price).

If you can't get an option, another way to tie up the property without buying it is to use an *assignment* of purchase. This is a bit trickier. Here you make an offer to purchase, usually for cash. However, when you make your offer, you state that the buyer is your name *or assigns*. What this means is that either you can buy the property or anyone else you assign the contract to can buy the property.

Buying with an Assignment

Many sellers will happily agree to an assigned contract. After all, they don't care who buys their property, so long as they get out with their money.

TRAP

Do *not* attempt an assignment without first consulting with an attorney for the rules in your state.   After you've done it a few times, you may be able to handle it on your own. But, when getting started, you definitely need legal assistance.

Some savvy sellers, however, won't agree to an "or assigns" sales contract. The reason is that they are afraid that you might not be able to get a needed mortgage and want a back door out or that you're planning to sell your contract to someone else (which is, in fact, the case!) and that person may not qualify for a needed mortgage. In other words, the assignment weakens the offer, and you have to be prepared for some sellers to refuse to sign.

In order to calm the seller's fears, you may need to put up a bigger deposit or avoid putting many escape clauses into the contract, which can increase your risks.

Unlike the option, the assignment runs for as long as you've got to close the deal, typically 30 to 45 days. That means that you've got to find a buyer and conclude your other end of the deal very quickly.

Hopefully you have done your homework and have a rebuyer waiting in the wings. You now make a separate agreement for the property with the rebuyer, but of course your sale is for a higher price. When the deal is ready to close, the rebuyer's name is substituted for yours on the deed.

Again, you never actually make the purchase. The transaction is basically handled in escrow. At the end of the deal, you get your money out, typically in cash.

Assignment Advantages

- You don't need much cash. You only have to put up the original deposit when you buy the property from the seller, and you get this back from your rebuyer.
- You don't own the property so you don't have to qualify or obtain a mortgage, make mortgage payments, pay taxes, or handle insurance, maintenance, or repairs.
- It's a quick deal. You can expect to get your profit out within 30 to 45 days.

Assignment Disadvantages

- You actually do commit to purchasing the property. If you can't go through with the deal for any reason, you can have an angry seller on your hands threatening a lawsuit. To protect yourself from having to complete the purchase in case you can't find a buyer (or your buyer falls through), you'll want lots of escape clauses. But escape clauses weaken your offer and lessen your chances of getting it accepted. So to make the deal, you may have to take a big risk.

- If the seller can't complete the sale for any number of reasons, you'll have an angry rebuyer on your hands threatening a lawsuit, so you'll again need lots of escape clauses to protect you from the rebuyer. Again, such clauses weaken your sales agreement.

Assignments have been used in real estate for as long as I can remember. However, as noted above, you need to include lots of escape clauses in the deal for your own protection.

Escape Clauses

Escape clause? What's that?

An *escape clause* is very commonly used in most real estate sales transactions. It's a clause that says the sale/purchase is "subject to" or "contingent upon" anything. If that anything happens, you can gracefully (without financial harm) back out of the deal. In modern transactions there are three widely accepted escape clauses that most sellers will agree to without blinking (and which won't weaken the transaction). These are the following:

Common Escape Clauses

---

1. **Finance contingency**—You have written into the contract that the deal is contingent upon your getting financing. No financing, no deal, and you're out without penalty. This usually runs for 30 days, but you must reasonably look for financing.
2. **Inspection contingency**—You must approve a professional inspector's report. Don't approve it, no deal. Usually you have 14 days to get the report and then either approve or disapprove it.
3. **Disclosure contingency**—You must approve the seller's disclosures. You don't approve them and there's no deal. But the time limit here is very short. In California, for example, it's statutorily three days (and the buyer can back out of the deal anytime during those three days by dis- approving).

The problem with these contingencies is that they probably don't offer you enough protection if you're doing an assignment. For example, in order to get the deal at a cut-rate price, you may have to offer the seller cash. In a cash sale, you don't have the protection of a finance contingency.

You might rely on the disclosure and professional inspection contingencies, but those usually run out after 14 days maximum. At that time you either agree to move forward without their protection, or back out of the deal. If you agree to move forward and something adverse happens (your rebuyer backs out), you're stuck for the house!

Trying to Limit Your Liability

Most investors who are flipping by using an assignment want to add other contingencies. This is easy to do, but not easy to get accepted.

You can make the sale contingent on anything: sunspots occurring within the next month, your winning the lottery, a snowstorm in Beverly Hills . . . anything at all. However, any contingency you add that's not reasonable (such as the three mentioned above) is likely to be considered frivolous by the seller and a reason not to sell to you. Thus, the more escape clauses you include, the less likely you are to get the seller to sign. And the fewer escape clauses you include, the greater your risk.

One possible way out of this conundrum is to use the "liquidated damages" clause found in most real estate contracts. If you sign this (and the seller does too), then the total amount of damages that you are likely to have to pay in the event you don't (or can't) make the deal is supposedly limited to your deposit. If you only put up a $1000 deposit, you may not have a great deal at risk.

However, don't rely on the liquidated damages clause. A nasty seller can hire an attorney to challenge it, and you could spend a lot more money defending yourself in court—and possibly lose.

Other investors form limited liability corporations in the hope of shielding themselves if problems occur. This may or may not work as the officers (owners) of the corporation may still be held liable in some cases.

Why All the Cautions?

The reason is that assigned purchase agreements tend to be rather iffy. There's a lot that can go wrong between signing them and actually concluding a sale between seller and rebuyer. If the sale can't be concluded, the seller is, of course, likely to get angry. And you want some good cover when that happens.

There's also an inherent problem in using an assignment to flip a property. It's this: most sellers have a kind of personal relationship with the buyer. They want to know who's buying their property. (This is even the case with banks, which almost always insist on knowing exactly with whom they're dealing.) Thus the sale is both business and personal. However, when you assign the purchase agreement, you break that personal bond. Most sellers, nevertheless, are willing to go along provided the deal concludes in a reasonable fashion. But, it's strictly business.

However, if they discover that you're reselling the property at a substantial hidden profit, most sellers are very unhappy. After all, they conclude, who are you to them (there's nothing personal here), and what are you bringing to the table? You're just a middleman. They feel that your profit should rightly go into their pockets.

Should it? Probably not. After all, if they could have sold for full price, they most certainly would have. What you're bringing to the transaction is your marketing expertise.

Nevertheless, you could have an angry seller on your hands, who at the least refuses to sign off on the deal unless he or she gets more money or at worst wants to back out of the deal or even take you to court. Thus, to oil the waters, many investors who flip in this manner just don't tell the seller. These investors believe that what the sellers don't know won't hurt them.

Therein lies the rub. When the sellers find out, as they often do, there's hell to pay.

Making Full Disclosure

TIP

There shouldn't be anything illegal or even unethical in flipping property, so long as all parties involved are made aware of what's happening.

However, when one party or another doesn't know what's going on, there's all kinds of opportunity for things to go wrong. Keeping secrets, in this case, can sink your ship. Remember, it shouldn't make any difference what you do with property after you and the seller agree on price. If you can flip it to another buyer for a better price, so be it.

The answer here is full disclosure. From the onset, let the buyer know what you're paying for the property (and get confirmation on a signed statement from the buyer). From the onset, let the seller know what you're going to sell it for (and get confirmation on a signed statement from the seller). It will help prevent either party from discovering this later, thinking you were trying to pull a fast one, and going after you. If either buyer or seller refuse to go along with the deal when you tell them your resell price and the deal doesn't go through, so be it. Better not to make a deal that will later get you into trouble.

Beware of Using Double Escrows to Conceal Information

A double escrow is sometimes used to facilitate a flip. However, it can also be used to deceive a buyer and a seller. It's where there are two escrows held simultaneously. In one you are the buyer, and in the other you are the seller. They close simultaneously— you buy the property from the seller in one and at the same time sell it to the rebuyer in the other. However, because they are separate, they can be used to conceal information from both the seller and the rebuyer.

If you give full disclosure, as previously noted, there's probably nothing wrong with using a double-escrow. However, if the seller only knows about one escrow and the buyer about another, there's not full disclosure. Indeed, because there are two separate escrows the other parties may be prevented from knowing the true nature of the deal.

It is most certainly illegal for a real estate agent to conduct a double escrow and receive an undisclosed profit from a property he or she is listing. It may not be illegal, but is certainly unethical for an investor to do the same thing. Full disclosure is necessary. The seller needs to know what the buyer is paying, and the buyer needs to know the profit you're making.

If you're worried about this, the sure way to avoid problems is to avoid double-escrowing a property.

Remember, the right way to handle a flip is to be sure that all parties know what you're doing (and get it in writing in case someone should later have an attack of memory failure). Quite often when they learn of it, they'll admire you for it. After all, remember that you're providing a sale for a seller who wants to get out. And you're providing a home for a buyer who wants to get in. Why shouldn't you be entitled to a profit for that? It's a win, win, win situation!

False Appraisals—the Bane of Flipping

What's given flipping a bad name more than anything else over the past few years are unscrupulous investors who have manipulated appraisals. Rather than do the real work of the transaction, namely finding properties that are selling below market, these unscrupulous investors have purchased properties at actual market and then, by obtaining falsely high appraisals (and, thus, falsely high mortgages), sold them for above market to unwary buyers. This has been done in apparent collusion with a few unscrupulous lenders and appraisers who helped secure higher appraisals than were warranted and made bigger loans than were justified. Often these properties were sold to poor minority or immigrant rebuyers who really didn't understand about market value or how high their payments would be. Subsequently, when these rebuyers couldn't make stiff payments, the houses were lost to foreclosure.

Almost all home mortgages are one way or another insured or guaranteed through the government or a government-related agency (FHA, VA, Fannie Mae, Freddie Mac, and so forth). When the government began taking these properties back, it found out what was happening and launched criminal investigations into the flippers.

This is not something you ever want to have happen to you. Always do the right thing. Find undervalued properties. There are more than enough of them out there to go around. Then, let everyone know what's happening in the deal, and get legitimate loans and appraisals. You'll do the seller, the rebuyer, the government, and even yourself a big favor.

Holding versus Flipping?

Now we've seen both sides of the coin—buy and then hold, waiting for prices to go up so that you can later resell for a big profit, or flipping to make a quick profit.

Once in a great while you'll find a property that you can either quickly flip or hold for the long term based on your assessment of its rental value. (See earlier chapters.) Should you flip or hold?

My answer has always been, "Whenever you can flip a property, do it. For every flippable property you find, you'll find half a dozen or more perfectly acceptable properties that you can hold. Finding holders is easy; finding flippers is hard."

Further, you need the cash that flipping can generate. Holding properties tends to drain cash away. Often there is some small negative cash flow, at least in the early years. And it may be a long time before you are able to get cash out of the holders in order to buy more properties.

The Bottom Line

It's not a question of should you flip or should you hold. You should do both, as circumstances dictate. You'll need the cash you can generate from a flippable property. And you'll need the eventual income and long-term equity gain you'll get from a holder.

9
Acquiring Rentals

The plan is simple: Acquire rentals over time (see Chapters 1 and 2). The execution, however, can be a bit more complicated.

Here we're going to look at your sources of good rental properties that can be purchased with little or no cash. That doesn't mean that all of these are available all of the time. Rather, like the "early bird that gets the worm," you'll need to be on your toes checking all of the sources on a regular basis to come up with good properties.

The good part, of course, is that you don't need many finds. One good rental every one or two years can make you wealthy over the long haul. And if you find a hot property that you can flip while checking these out, so much the better!

Begin at the Beginning

Normally there are so many properties listed for sale with agents at any given time that there are always many that would serve as good rentals that you can buy with little to no cash. The trick, of course, is to separate the wheat from the chaff—to separate the properties suitable for you from all of the others. So begin by contacting agents and explaining just what you're looking for: a good rental property that you can buy with little to no cash.

Don't expect every agent to be helpful. Finding a home without a big down payment to work with can be a tough job, and many agents would simply prefer to work easier deals. That's why I suggest contacting a number of agents until you find one who knows exactly what you want and is willing to work with you.

Don't think such an agent doesn't exist. A really smart agent will realize that as you become successful, he or she will gain success as well. After all, think how many commissions are involved if you buy a property every year or two for 20 years? All an agent really needs is a handful of good clients like you to make a decent living.

Also, don't worry that the agent will snatch a good property out from under you. Every agent I've ever known would much rather get a commission, which means immediate income, than buy a listed property, which means long-term investment. Agents need that constant influx of cash that commissions supply to survive. Normally, they only buy for investment as a last resort.

You'll want to work with an agent who has access to the MLS (Multiple Listing Service) in your area. These are usually members of the NAR (National Association of Realtors©).

Remember, be sure your agent understands that you need nothing-down financing (as well as little-to-no closing costs). If you explain that you're going to be living in the property, it will all become much easier. (When dealing with properties in higher-priced areas, consider looking out of the immediate area. See Chapter 6.)

Tell your agent exactly what you're interested in. You'll have your choice of the greatest selection of properties on the MLS. Having said that, here are three good tips on the types of property to look for in the agent's listing book.

What to Look for in the Listings

Listings That Are Stale

Usually these are the properties that have been listed the longest. A seller who puts a property on the market on Wednesday isn't likely to cut his price by the following Monday. On the other hand, a seller who's had her property on the market for three months with no activity is likely to be very anxious to make a deal . . . and cut her price to do it. In other words, look for the "stale" listings, those that have been out there the longest.

A typical listing is for 90 days. As you get closer to the end of that time, the agent is more likely to put pressure on the seller to accept any offer. After all, unless the seller decides to renew, after 90 days the agent has lost the listing and a commission.

In a normal market, a large number of properties will be in the stale category. Indeed, most properties will take two months or more to sell. In a slow market, you'll want to extend your time frame to homes that have gone unsold for six months or longer. In a hot market, however, you will have to reduce that time frame, sometimes to a few weeks.

Listings That Have Expired

A listing that doesn't sell goes "off the books." This doesn't mean that it disappears. It just means that it's no longer carried in the computer as an active listing. But it is on a list somewhere.

Typically agents can pull these expired listings. (The agents often use them as a source of possible new listings for themselves.) Check them over carefully. Sometimes, lost among them is a gem. This is typically a property where the price was reduced several times and where the old listing described the owner as "highly motivated." You might find a property where the owner is still desperate to sell, but simply has given up and doesn't know how to do it. Have your agent contact the seller, get a short-term (one day) listing, and show you the property.

If it looks good, try a low-ball offer. It's not always going to work. But, then again, you don't need to get a hit very often to win the game.

Price Reductions

A seller who cuts the price by $500 is merely trying to attract attention. A seller who cuts the price by $20,000 is serious. Multiple price reductions indicate a very anxious seller, particularly when the reductions come close to one another. When you find a property that has been reduced in price and which otherwise seems suitable, don't feel you have to offer the current asking price. Just because a seller has reduced the price doesn't mean it's at rock bottom. Treat a reduced price as you would any other, as the starting point for negotiations. Work down from there.

Read the Listings Carefully

Listing agents will try to convey the seller's motivation in the listing. Look for phrases such as "highly motivated" or "bring in all offers," or "wants to move immediately." You get the idea. The agent is sending out the word that this seller is very anxious and will consider low-ball offers. If this is combined with price reductions, you probably have a real opportunity in the making.

What about Getting a License and Avoiding the Real Estate Agent Altogether?

We've already discussed this in Chapter 5, but it comes up as a question so often that the answer is worth reiterating. There's nothing wrong with getting a license and joining the local Real Estate Board in order to promote your own real estate activities. There's nothing wrong with making your own offers on homes and, if you earn it, collecting the buyer's agent's commission. However, upon reflection, it may not be worthwhile.

It takes some studying and effort to get a license, and then, assuming it's a salesperson's license, you have to get a broker to take you on. That means that even if you buy a property for yourself and earn a commission, part of it will go to the broker.

Further, it costs money to join and maintain membership in a local Real Estate Board. You probably will find the costs prohibitive if you only want to find and buy a property every year or two.

Finally, it can be very difficult to get the best financing when you're an agent. Lenders simply are always suspicious when an agent buys the property, and they typically want to see that buyer put in some of his or her own cash.

All of which is to say that you might actually be better off without that real estate license (although learning all you can about the field is certainly worthwhile).

TIP

There's no reason not to ask for a discount on the commission when you're using the same agent year in and year out. After all, you're making him or her lots of money, and he or she will very likely want to keep you happy.

Do the Legwork Yourself on "By Owner" Properties

Many beginning investors make the mistake of assuming that all properties are listed. That's not the case. Roughly 10 to 15 percent of homes for sale are FSBOs or "for sale by owner" properties. Since there's no agent involved, you can easily contact the owner yourself and determine if one of these is just right for you.

While FSBOs are advertised, really the best way to find them is to drive around the neighborhoods in which you're interested. Think of this as your "farm." Define certain neighborhoods and, on a fairly regular basis, drive or walk them. Look for signs that indicate a person is selling a home FSBO.

Another good source for FSBOs in your area is to check the Internet. Today, virtually every property that's listed with an agent or that is being sold FSBO is also listed somewhere on the Internet. Listed property can be found on sites such as *www.realtor.com* (operated in cooperation with the NAR—National Association of Realtors) or *www.cyberhomes.com.*

FSBO sites come and go. Your best bet is to check out one of the search engines such as Yahoo or Google and simply write in the keyword FSBO. You'll immediately be given dozens of suggestions that offer listings from direct sellers.

Working the Internet can be enticing. After all, you don't even have to leave your own home. You can view images of almost all houses that are available. (Sometimes even virtual tours are available.) You get a detailed description of the property as well as its location, including a map showing how to get there. And you're usually given the e-mail address and phone number of the seller. You can communicate with the seller directly by e-mail. Thus, you can very quickly scan dozens if not hundreds of listing from the comfort of your computer room. This tends to be far more efficient than trying to look at a listing book in an agent's office. It's certainly more efficient than touring streets hunting for FSBO signs.

On the other hand, there are downsides to using an Internet listing. You don't actually see the property or neighborhood on your computer. As of this writing you still cannot easily make binding offers over the Web.

So the Internet is basically a good source of locating FSBOs. But it's only a first step. Once you find a property you like, you should go to see it. And then you can carry on just as if you discovered it by walking your neighborhood.

When you find a FSBO that looks suitable, stop by and engage the seller/owner in discussion. Find out what the asking price is and any special features. Then check it out. Do a CMA (comparative market analysis). Here you compare the FSBO to other recent sales to see whether the price is right. (Often it's too high. Chances are you'll find that the FSBO price is higher than market price—sellers typically think they can sell their property for more when they do it on their own.)

However, occasionally you'll find a FSBO seller who sees the light. He or she will price their home below market in order to attract buyers. Rather than attempt to save a commission, this seller will give the commission to the buyer (in the form of a lower price) in order to get a faster sale. This is someone with whom you can reason—and negotiate.

This is not to say that you should immediately pay the full asking price, even if it is below market. You should still negotiate, even low-ball. But it's a much better place from which to start than a seller who thinks the property is so wonderful that you ought to pay full price for it.

TRAP

Buying FSBO is more difficult. You don't have an agent to handle the paperwork and other details.

Further, once you find a property you like, go back to the Internet for additional help. You can find Web sites to help you locate comparable properties sold in the neighborhood and get information on schools and crime, title reports, and home inspectors. It's simply a matter of locating a Web site that caters to what you need. Two that I have found helpful in terms of providing investor services are *www.dataquick.com* and *www.lendingtree.com*.

Check Out Bank-Owned Properties

Lenders take back lots of properties because borrower/owners for one reason or another can't make the payments. These properties are typically called REOs, or real estate owned. They show up as a liability on the books of a lender rather than as a performing mortgage, which would be an asset. Therefore, lenders are very anxious to get rid of REOs. However, not so anxious that they're willing to sell to just anyone. They want to be sure that the next buyer/owner doesn't likewise default.

This means that if you don't have cash to put down, it's harder (but not impossible) to buy an REO. What's involved is simply confronting the lender with your situation. If you have no cash, but good credit, a deal might just be made. Or, if you have no cash and less than perfect credit, if the property is a real dog that the lender desperately wants to dump, a deal can still be made. In REOs, very frequently the lender is the one who will finance the deal, so it has a lot of flexibility in determining how much down payment it will require and to whom it will sell the property.

TIP

REOs can be wonderful opportunities. The trick is finding out about them.

Almost universally, lenders won't admit publicly that they have a REO problem. Many won't admit they even have any REOs. Thus, you can't usually just walk in and ask to buy one.

This certainly seems to work against a lender's best interests, at least on the surface. One would think that they would be out there advertising those properties as heavily as possible. Yet, they don't. Do you ever recall seeing a lender advertising under its own name for REO buyers? Except for auction sales in extremely bad markets, it normally just doesn't happen. (Most of the public isn't even familiar with the term REO.)

The reason it doesn't happen is basically twofold. A lender doesn't want to alert federal watchdogs that it has a REO problem. Keeping up a good face can mean the difference between remaining in business or being considered insolvent. Also, depositors are wary about where they place their money. They might just bolt if they thought the lender was shaky because it owned too many foreclosed properties.

The truth is that although lenders keep quiet about REOs as far as the general public is concerned, they are often open about them to legitimate investors. After all, they do want to sell them in order to get the money invested back at work as a mortgage.

Basically you need to let a lender know that you are a sophisticated investor and that you understand what an REO is and you'd like to bid on one. Once the lender understands that you're special and not part of the public only interested in deposits, it will open up, at least in a limited way. Therefore, you need to call the lender and ask for the officer who deals with REOs. Sometimes you'll be told that this particular lender handles all REOs through a specific real estate broker. You'll have to contact the broker. Other times you'll learn that the lender handles them itself and there's a list. You'll want to get the list.

Bank Fixer Uppers

It's common to find REOs in distressed condition. When you get to the REO it may still be in the terrible shape in which the lender got it back from a borrower/owner who bailed.

TIP

When you find an REO in distressed condition, don't turn your head away in disgust. You're not looking at a disaster. You may be looking at an opportunity.

If you're willing to do the scratch work of bringing the property back into shape, the lender may be willing to stretch to give you a particularly high loan.

Of course, many lenders will fix up their REOs. When they do, however, they typically expect top dollar and strong buyers.

Whether a fixer upper or refurbished, most REOs are sold "as is," even if the lender handles the financing. The lender/seller usually makes no warranty to you of any kind. This means that if you discover a problem after the sale that costs $10,000 to fix, it's your headache, not the lender's. (That's why the price is cheaper!)

While most states now require sellers to provide disclosure statements, this may not apply to a lender that may be federally chartered. The lender may refuse to give you any kind of disclosure statement. Or, if you do get disclosures, they may disclose virtually nothing with the lender claiming it knows nothing about the property. Once again, you're on your own.

Certainly, you'll want to get a home inspection. You'll want the most thorough inspector you can find. However, don't expect the lender to do anything toward correcting problems the inspector finds. Typically, beyond basic refurbishing, most lenders will make no repairs of any kind, even if the inspector finds a safety issue. (In that case, the lender may insist you sign a statement that you accept the property at your own risk.)

Consider Foreclosures

Most people have also heard that if you can pick up a property in foreclosure, you stand to make a good profit. There are perils in foreclosures, however. Also, it can be difficult to purchase one without cash. After all, many foreclosure sales are for cash only. Therefore, it's vital to arrange for financing *before* looking at foreclosed properties.

There are two occasions when you can buy a property in foreclosure (besides after the bank has foreclosed and it becomes an REO, as described previously). The first is when the property goes into default.

- **Default**—The seller has stopped making payments (the most common reason for default), and the lender has given notice that the foreclosure process has begun. You must buy the property from the owner/borrower. This is very tricky and should only be done with the aid of a competent and experienced attorney.

- **Foreclosure Sale**—After a prescribed period of time and after going through all the legal steps for foreclosing as required by your state, the property is sold to the highest bidder "on the court house steps." Again, you must know how to bid and what the requirements are. You must also have checked out the property on your own. Again I suggest you only attempt this with the aid of a competent and experienced agent or attorney.

Sometimes foreclosures are listed on the MLS. Other times the owner will have a "by owner" sign on the front. Other sources include title insurance companies, which act as trustees in foreclosure. They will often provide a list of the foreclosures they are handling.

In addition, there's almost always a legal newspaper (one that carries legal notices) in every area in which foreclosure notices are published. Pick this up, and you may be able to find every foreclosure in town. Be aware, however, that frequently only the *legal* description of the property is given, not the street address. You can get this converted at the county assessor's office, but it is a hassle.

Also, most larger metropolitan areas have foreclosure bulletins. These are private publications that list all foreclosures and give street addresses, names, dates, and so forth. They are everything you need. However, it usually costs a lot, typically several hundred dollars a year to subscribe.

Finally, there are a number of Web sites that deal almost exclusively in foreclosures and REOS. When using a Web site, however, be sure to check that the foreclosure is indeed in your area.

Buying When the Owner Is in Default

Once you find someone who is in foreclosure, it's now up to you to contact him or her directly and find out if there is a good deal available for you. Hopefully you already have a name and phone number. Now, just give this person a call. Explain that you're an investor and that you're looking for property in the area.

What you can offer to the owner is to make up the back payments and penalties and save the owner's credit rating in exchange for the title to the property. In other words, you can offer to take it over. The advantage here is that you get the property for virtually no money down plus whatever equity the owner may have. The disadvantage is that the loan may not be assumable. If that's the case, you may have to not only make up back payments and penalties but also secure a new loan with accompanying points and fees.

In short, it may cost you many thousands of dollars to take over this property and bail out this owner. Therefore, be sure you know that you can get full financing before you begin. Otherwise, with little to no cash, it's simply going to be wasted time and effort on your part. Also, be aware that some states give special protection to sellers in default. Even though they sell it to you in an arm's-length deal, they just might be able to come back as much as a year or more later and demand that you return it to them! This can be particularly unpleasant if you've spent time and money improving the property. Check with your state's real estate division for the rules that could affect you.

It's important that you calculate all the costs of taking over a property in default including back payments, penalties and interest on the mortgage, the cost of new financing, and any refurbishing that may be necessary to put the property in shape to rent out. I suspect that most of the time you'll find it simply doesn't pencil out—it's not worth it. However, once in awhile you'll find a real gem here, and that makes it all worthwhile.

TRAP

 You should try to get title insurance when you buy a foreclosure. This allows you protection against many of the perils of an "off the books" sale, such as letting you know who actually owns the property, how many loans are on it, what their balances are, and so on.

Knowledge is king. Without a good title search, you might end up paying a lot of money for a property where the debt is higher than the value. Also, some states offer owners a kind of redemption period if they sell their houses while in foreclosure. Check in your area. If it exists, it could mean the seller could come back even years later and stake a claim on the property!

Buying at the Foreclosure Sale

At the time of the foreclosure sale, the lender offers the full price of the mortgage (or trust deed) plus allowable expenses (penalties, interest, and so on) in order to buy the property. But there is nothing to prevent you or anyone else from offering more and buying the property yourself.

Your offer, however, usually must be in the form of cash, so you will have to work out financing in advance. And you will often receive no title insurance or other guarantees as to the status of the property. (You might, for example, think you're bidding on a first mortgage only to find that it's a second or third. This could be catastrophic for you.)

All of which is to say you should check the property out thoroughly before considering making an offer. Try to get title insurance. And certainly get the aid of someone who has experience in buying property at auction, such as an agent or attorney who specializes in the field.

HUD-Owned Properties

HUD (Housing and Urban Development Department) repos can be an excellent opportunity to buy a home, if you're short on cash. They offer the property at little or no money down and sometimes can fold the closing costs into the mortgage.

However, to get this excellent financing, you *must* intend to live in the property, as described in Chapter 3. If you buy as an investor, HUD almost always insists on 10 percent down plus closing costs.

At any given time HUD may have tens of thousands of repossessed homes for sale across the country. You can search for HUD homes in your area on the Internet at *www.hud.gov/local/sams.ctznhome.html.*

Since the homes come back mainly through the FHA program, and since that program has a maximum loan amount as of this writing of around $240,000, you're not likely to find many upscale properties here. Most are going to be in the moderate-to-low price range.

Additionally, they may not be in the best condition. HUD usually does not fix up the properties. That means that they may be in anywhere from average to really bad shape. Don't be surprised at the terrible condition in which you may find a HUD home. Remember, the former owner lost the property to foreclosure. There was little incentive to keep it up. Additionally, since that time there may have been vandalism.

- **Making an Offer**—You must make your offer through an agent who represents HUD in your local area. Once you locate a home that you're interested in, contact the referred agent and go see the property. The agent can arrange to have you walk through. You'll also make your offer directly through the agent. HUD tries to sell its homes at fair market price.

- **Financing**—HUD doesn't make loans directly, but it does work with lenders in a variety of programs. As noted, you may be able to get in with virtually nothing down, so long as you're intending to occupy the home. If you're looking for both a house to live in *and* a long-term investment, this can be the perfect choice for you.

- **Special Terms**—If the home is in bad shape, HUD may offer a fix-up allowance. This can be either in the form of an additional price reduction, or a special fix-up loan. However, in order to get this, you must be sure it's part of your purchase offer. Once you've made your offer and it's accepted by HUD, it's too late to demand a fix-up allowance. HUD may also offer special incentives if it's particularly interested in moving a property. For owner-occupants this can include a moving allowance

- **Due Diligence**—You'll want to have a professional inspection of the home. However, unlike conventional purchases where the professional inspection is normally conducted *after* you've signed a purchase agreement with the seller, with HUD you'll need to make your inspection *beforehand.* HUD doesn't like to tie up homes on contingencies that involve inspections.

VA-Owned Properties

VA (Veteran's Administration) repos, like those of HUD, can be an excellent purchase opportunity, so long as you plan on occupying the property. Unlike HUD, which insures loans to lenders, the VA *guarantees* the performance of a loan to a lender. VA repos often include built-in financing.

To purchase a VA home, as with the HUD program, you usually must go through a local real estate agent who represents the VA's property management program. Typically these agents will advertise in local newspapers. You may also find most, but not all, of them listed on the VA's property management Web site. Unlike HUD, the VA does not maintain an Internet presence with a list of all properties. It is up to the local property management office to determine whether to link to the VA site and whether to list its homes on the Web. Check out *www.homeloans.va.gov/homes.html.*

In order to make an actual offer, you must go through an agent and use the proper forms.

As with HUD homes, many of the VA properties are in the same condition as when they were turned over after foreclosure. In the past, however, the VA has had an extensive program of refurbishing properties in order to get a higher value. If you buy a refurbished home, don't expect to get any kind of bargain on the price. How the homes are handled is largely determined by the regional VA property management office.

Again, you'll want to have a professional inspection so that you'll know what you're getting. However, as with HUD, you'll need to conduct the inspection during the offering period and not after you have your offer accepted. The agent who's handling the house can arrange for you and your inspector to get in. Be sure you use a sharp pencil when you calculate how much the property is really worth.

The VA program has been in existence for over 50 years. I've been involved with it at different times and in different ways and have seen many owners obtain solid properties through it.

Secondary Lenders' Properties

Fannie Mae along with Freddie Mac (discussed next) are the main secondary lenders in the country. They underwrite most of the conventional (nongovernment insured or guaranteed) mortgages that are made. Each year they take back thousands of properties (both houses and condos) through repossession and then offer them for sale.

As with HUD and the VA, Fannie Mae requires you to go through a local real estate agent. However, the agents are required to list all the homes on the local MLS, so there's no difficulty in gaining access. Typically any agent in the local Board can show you the home, as well as make the offer for you. Your offer will then go to the listing agent who will in turn present it to Fannie Mae.

You'll have to come up with your own financing here, so check once again into Chapter 3 for low-down/no-down mortgages.

You can find a list of Fannie Mae homes at its Web site *www.fanniemae.com/homes.html.*

Freddie Mac, like Fannie Mae, offers single-family detached, condos, and townhomes. However, Freddie Mac generally cleans and fixes up its homes before offering them for sale. If you want to submit an offer on a home that involves doing the fix-up work yourself, chances are Freddie Mac will still at the least clean up the property before you buy it.

Through its HomeSteps program, Freddie Mac will offer homes to owner-occupants at competitive interest rates with 5 percent low down payments and no mortgage insurance. It will also offset some of the title and escrow costs. These homes are almost all competitively priced at market.

Freddie Mac homes are offered through a select group of lenders. To find out more about them, check into *www.homesteps.com.*

Other Government Repo Programs

There are many other government repo programs including some from the IRS as well as local government authorities. Here's a list you may find helpful in checking them out.

Department of Veteran Affairs—*www.homeloans.va.gov/homes.htm*

Federal Deposit Insurance Corporation—*www.fdic.gov/buying/ owner/index.html*

GSA—*http://propertydisposal.gsa.gov/property/propforsale/*

TIP

You're best off checking these out at their Web sites. If you call, you could spend hours trying to reach the right person with the correct information. The Web sites, on the other hand, are generally organized to give you the information you need right away.

Keep in mind that in all of these programs, the government would prefer to sell to a buyer who comes in with cash. If you have little to no cash, you'll have to make that clear at the onset and see if the program offers some special financing that can fit your needs or arrange financing through a mortgage broker beforehand.

10

The Keys to Being a Successful Landlord

If you're going to invest in real estate, you're going to be a landlord. It just goes with the territory.

If you don't want to be a landlord, I'll understand. You may previously have had a bad experience either with a tenant or as a tenant.

However, even if this is the case I encourage you to read these keys. They may clear up many misconceptions that you've had. And at the same time, they may give you insight into what it is to be a landlord.

I've owned property for many decades and been a landlord most of that time. Rarely have I had a bad experience. I've enjoyed most of the tenants I've had, and I hope they've enjoyed having me as a landlord. Yes, it's a business. But, if handled fairly and equitably, it can be a win–win business.

TIP

 Always remember that the tenant's rent is paying for your mortgage and other expenses—in short, it's making you rich over time.

Keep in mind that you won't learn how to be a good landlord from reading one chapter in a book and you should talk with other landlords as well as check out books detailing the subject. Further, the entire field of landlord-tenant relations is filled with pitfalls including many legal requirements and time limits. Be sure to get a good rental attorney to work with and help you get started.

Key #1—Remember, Business Is Business

The ideals of generosity and equality are something we Americans celebrate. As a result, I have seen first-time landlords bend over backward to cater to the whims of their tenants. They accept late rents and provide unreasonable services—all in the desire to prove that they are truly generous and to make their tenants feel equal. Along the way they stop renting aggressively and usually end up paying for it financially.

The truth is that the landlord is in a much more financially demanding position than the tenant. As the landlord you own the property. You stand to reap all the profits if values go up and to lose a significant amount of money if they go down. You also have all the responsibilities of paying taxes, insurance, and mortgage interest, as well as paying for repairs. The tenant has none of those responsibilities. He or she only has to get the rent in on time and keep the place reasonably clean and tidy.

Because of the different responsibilities, you can never be on the same level as the tenant. The property is always going to mean more to you than the tenant. And you are always going to have to be in the position of holding tenants to the terms of tenancy they agreed to.

In short, renting property is not democracy in action. It's a business. You're more like a CEO, and the tenant is more like an employee.

While this analogy is helpful, it's important not to stretch it too far. To counter tyrannical and unfair treatment by some landlords, the courts over the years have strengthened tenants' rights to the point where today many landlords feel the tenants have the upper hand. In most states the landlord is so restricted in what he or she can or can't do that some people say it just isn't worth renting out property any more.

I don't find that to be true. To my way of thinking, the courts and the legislatures have simply given tenants protections from unscrupulous landlords that they needed. If you're not unscrupulous, you should have little to worry about.

The whole point of this discussion is to note the importance of striking the right tone in your relationship with a tenant. You can't be arbitrary or dictatorial. Yet you can't be a wimp either.

You have to be in charge. It's your property, and how you handle the tenant will largely determine what happens to it. Get your head straight. The tenant is not doing you a favor by renting from you. He or she needs shelter and has to rent from someone. On the other hand, you're not doing the tenant a favor. There are lots of other rentals.

Remember, it's a business and should be run as such. You're the boss and, within the law, you set up the rules and see that they are followed. Keep to that thinking and you should do well.

Pick up a list of landlord/tenant laws appropriate to your state, and study it before you begin renting. While the rules may differ from state to state, in almost all cases they are quite clear, and you don't want to break them. A tenant lawsuit is no fun for anyone.

Key #2—Offer a Clean Rental

The biblical observation "As you sow, so shall you reap" really does apply here. If the property you rent is clean when the tenant moves in, the chances are very good it will be clean when the tenant moves out.

This should be obvious, but it really isn't. I have known many landlords who really don't care what their property looks like. Their attitude seems to be, "I'm not going to live there, so what do I care? Let the tenants clean it if they want!"

That's not a very charitable attitude, and it often comes from having a tenant who leaves the property a mess. However, having once been burned does not mean you need to fear fire. (It was Mark Twain who observed that a cat that jumps on a hot stove will never jump on a hot one again, or a cold one either for that matter.)

Dirty and messy properties take far longer to rent, command lower rents, and attract a much lower quality tenant. The person you really hurt when you fail to clean up your rental is you.

I always go through a rental and clean the carpets and floors and make sure the kitchen is spotless, with the stove, refrigerator (if any), and sink shiny and clean. I also repaint the walls as necessary. When prospective tenants walk in, I want them to think they are getting a place that's as good as new. That way, hopefully, they'll take pride in living there and will take care of it.

Sometimes when a property has a lot of tenants moving through it, it begins to take on a shabby appearance. After a while the landlord tires of spending the money and time to clean it after each tenant and, instead, offers to pay for the paint and cleaning equipment if the tenant will do the clean-up work. This works only in a very limited way. If the property is already cleaned up but a little bit on the worn side, and the tenant wants a gallon of paint to touch up a bedroom, by all means buy the paint. You probably have a very clean tenant who will take good care of the property. On the other hand, if the place is a mess and the tenant wants a gallon of paint to fix it up, don't buy the paint. Have the place fixed up before you go looking for a tenant. I've tried it both ways, and I've found that tenants who are willing to rent a place that is a mess, even if they are willing to clean it up a bit, will still turn out to be poor quality tenants who have trouble making rent payments and who leave the place even worse.

Good tenants simply won't accept rentals that are a mess. They won't want to spend much time (with the occasional exception of the fastidious tenant noted above) cleaning. They know they are good tenants, they know they can find a clean place, and they will skip yours. As a result, you get what's left—the type of tenant you don't want.

If you do buy paint for tenants or otherwise allow them to fix up the place, be sure that you choose the paint, wallpaper, or whatever. Always select the best possible quality (so it will last) and the most generic colors (so they will appeal to the most people). If you let the tenant make the selection you could end up with a purple bathroom and a red living room.

Key #3—Take Care of the Water Bill

In most rentals the tenant pays the utility bills. This includes gas or oil, electricity, phone, and water. This is almost certainly the case with single-family residences where everything is separately metered.

There's nothing wrong with this, unless you live in an arid climate and have a lot of landscaping. That landscaping will need water, and in arid climates water tends to be expensive. Don't expect any tenant to go out of his or her way to pay a big water bill to help your landscaping. Yes, most tenants do like nice landscaping. No, most tenants won't pay extra for it.

The answer is a water allowance. It doesn't have to be much. It doesn't even have to equal the costs the tenant will pay for all the water actually used. It's just the idea that you're contributing. Each time the tenant thinks about not watering, he or she will remember that allowance, not get angry about the cost, and water.

It doesn't work for every tenant, but it does work for many and could save you a lot of costs in relandscaping later on.

If you have large yards in front and back, you may want to consider providing a gardener. You often can charge more rent with a gardener, so there could be almost no cost to you, and it can mean keeping the property in great shape. If the property has a pool, a pool maintenance service is a must. Never rely on a tenant to take care of a pool.

Key #4—Know Whom You're Renting To

As suggested earlier, the way to get a tenant to take care of the property and pay the rent on time is to rent to the right tenant in the beginning. This is the biggest problem area for most new landlords. How do you get the right tenants?

Rest assured there is no guaranteed formula. There are, however, certain tips that will prove helpful.

Of course you will want to talk with the prospective tenants and form an opinion of them. (This is very important and is why I always suggest that you do the renting of the property personally.) Here are two critical areas to consider.

The Credit Report

Today, you as a landlord should have no trouble in getting a written credit report on a prospective tenant. All that you really need to do is to contact one of the local credit agencies (listed in your phone book), explain what you want, and have them send you some of their forms. The cost is usually under $25 for a brief report.

When you find likely tenant candidates, have them fill out the form, *being sure they give you permission to check their credit history.* Then contact the credit-reporting agency with your request. Usually within a day you'll have a printout of their credit history. Check it over carefully.

TRAP

 Avoid discrimination! To ensure that you're not accused of discrimination in renting, be sure you give everyone who comes by a rental application and the opportunity to fill it out. Antidiscrimination rules prohibit discriminating in rentals or advertising to rent on the basis of:

Race

Color

Religion

National origin or ancestry

Sex

Familial status

Physical disability

Ideally you're looking for tenants with no bad credit. They pay all their bills on time and have credit with a wide variety of lenders from credit card companies to department stores to banks. Chances are, however, you won't find this kind of tenant all the time (or even very often). More likely the person who rents has spotty credit—some good, some bad.

Study the credit report. If the prospective tenants have a lot of "late paying" notes, chances are your rent won't be paid on time either. If they have some loan defaults or other failures to pay, you may not get your rent at all.

The credit report should be taken as an indication of how the prospective tenants view their credit. If they view it casually and don't really care, then you could end up with no rent. You want tenants who take their credit seriously and who regularly pay on time. One of the biggest mistakes is to "fall in love" with a tenant (not literally, but figuratively). The tenant seems ideal, until the credit report comes in. You look at the bad credit report and then choose to ignore it because you're so convinced the tenant is wonderful. Bad move.

Ultimately it's a judgment call. However, if you decide not to give a bad credit report a lot of credence, why did you order the credit report in the first place?

Give the tenant a chance to explain bad credit. Listen to the explanation. It may be perfectly logical and may not be the tenant's fault.

Previous Landlords' Recommendations

To me, this is the single most important indicator of future tenant success. It's absolutely vital that you get the accurate name and phone number of the tenants' former landlords. It's a must that you get not just the previous landlord, but those going back two or three rentals. (If you just ask for the current landlord, you might get a wonderful recommendation from a landlord who's just dying to get rid of a tenant!)

Be sure you get written permission on your rental application from the perspective tenant. Then call up the former landlords, and ask them about the tenant. Explain that you are planning to rent your property to this tenant. Ask for a recommendation.

Some landlords are pleased to tell you all they know. Others are hesitant to talk for fear that anything they say may later be used against them by the tenant. (Just as in employer/employee relationships, there have been cases where tenants have sued former landlords over bad recommendations.)

If the landlord is hesitant to volunteer information, you can ask questions that will get you the answers you want. For example:

"Would you rent again to this tenant? Why not?"

"Would you charge a higher cleaning/security deposit next time? Why?"

"Would you allow this tenant to have a pet?"

In nearly all cases you can quickly find out what you need to know from the former landlord. Listen carefully to what's said. Usually the former landlord has no axe to grind, unless the tenant skipped without paying rent. Then the landlord may bend your ear telling you what a turkey the tenant was.

The credit report and former landlord recommendations are the two best sources of information about your prospective tenants. Don't skip either. They are important.

My Own Experiences

Having given you the rules about credit reports and former landlords' recommendations, let me say that I've broken them as well as kept them. I've rented to tenants with horrific credit reports. And I've rented to tenants whose former landlords told horror stories about them.

Why? A lot has to do with gut feelings and the tenants' explanations. In one case I rented to a tenant who explained her bad credit was because of a boyfriend who left her with a lot of bills. It turned out to be the truth, and she was a great tenant. In another case I rented to a tenant whose former landlord said he left the place a mess with real damage done and never paid the rent on time. The tenant explained that he left it clean and paid the rent on time, but the former landlord was mad because he moved out over a dispute about painting. The former landlord had promised to repaint the inside of the house and reneged. I believed the tenant and, again, he turned out to be great.

As I said, it's a judgment call.

Key #5—Don't Try to Avoid Children or Pets

This seems to fly in the face of advice that most landlords give (and that I gave earlier). They tell you to avoid renting to tenants with children whenever possible (under federal antidiscrimination rules, you cannot refuse to rent because a tenant has children) and avoid pets like the plague. Both can do damage to the property.

That is certainly true. However, the most reliable tenants tend to be the ones with kids. Family people tend to take care of property and pay the rent on time. If you try to avoid renting to people with kids, you may eliminate your best source of tenants.

Instead of not taking kids, try to rent to people who don't have more kids than the house can hold. A three-bedroom, two-bath house can easily accommodate two or three kids. It will, however, show wear and tear with six kids. (Also, be aware that small children are sometimes terrible tenants since they tend to write on the walls in crayon, which won't come off and is very difficult to paint over.)

You really don't have a choice. Depending on the circumstances, it is probably discrimination to deny a rental to a prospective tenant because of the fact that there are children in the family.

In the case of dogs, I follow the philosophy of an old friend who manages over 150 single-family residences. He says, "People always lie about keeping dogs. They always say they don't have any, and then, once they move in, the dog appears. So what's the point of saying no dogs in the rental agreement? Are you going to throw out a good tenant because he or she "acquires" a dog?

"As a result, I simply say that one dog is okay. If there end up being two, I look the other way. If there's a kennel, of course, I throw them out."

Cats and birds are something else. Cats that are not properly house trained may urinate on carpets. Cat urine is virtually impossible to get out. It may result in the need to get new padding under the carpeting, new carpets themselves, or even new flooring under the padding and the carpet! I always get a heftier cleaning deposit for a cat.

Birds can make a mess, and they can leave a peculiar odor in the house that is hard, but not impossible, to remove. Also, birds can sometimes screech loudly at odd times during the day or night disturbing others. I'd think twice about renting to a tenant with birds.

Key #6—Don't Always Try to Get the Last Month's Rent

This must certainly fly in the face of advice that most people have received. A lease that dictates that a landlord gets the first and last month's rent has been the traditional rental agreement. To now suggest that a landlord not go for it might be tantamount to criticizing mom, baseball, and apple pie.

Yet, my advice is not to go for first and last month's rent. Here's why.

The traditional lease in which the tenant pays the first and last month's rent grew mainly out of commercial usage. It's the sort of agreement you would use if you were renting a building to a commercial tenant. If the tenant didn't pay the rent on time, you could sue to collect the rent, and you would always be one month ahead by collecting that last month's rent up front.

With a single-family house, however, realistically you're never going to sue to collect rent from a tenant who is in the premises and who isn't paying. You're simply going to want to get that tenant out and someone better in. Suing is the last thing you want to do. (You'll sue for unlawful detainer—eviction—when the tenant doesn't leave and doesn't pay, and you might hope to recoup the lost rent later as a result of that suit.)

There's another problem with first and last month's rent. What you are mainly interested in (besides collecting rent) is that the tenant leave the property in as good a shape as he or she found it. First and last month's rent doesn't address that issue. A security/cleaning deposit does. Yet, if you've already collected first and last month's rent, how large a security deposit can you realistically hope to get? For example, if the rent is $1000 a month, first and last month's rent comes to $2000. How much more can you expect a tenant to pay for a security deposit—$200, $500? You reach a point where your property requires too much cash up front for any likely tenant to afford it.

A better way is to forgo the last month's rent paid in advance and instead get a very large cleaning/security deposit. Today, most savvy landlords are insisting on a security deposit at least equal to one month's rent if not more. If the property rents for $1000 a month, before moving in the tenant would be required to come up with $1000 first month's rent plus at least another $1000 or $1500 in a security deposit.

Some states limit the size of a security/cleaning deposit. The maximum you can charge may only be one and a half to two times a month's rent.

The tenant who puts up that much money has something substantial to lose if the property isn't left clean. And if the tenant doesn't pay, the deposit can always be used to compensate for lost rent. A last month's rent cannot be used as a cleaning deposit. (Check with the laws in your state to be sure that security deposits can be combined with cleaning deposits and used for either reason.)

One concern is the savvy tenant who doesn't make the last month's rent payment. When you call, the tenant says, "Please use the cleaning/security deposit."

You can write in the rental agreement that the cleaning/security deposit is *not* to be used as the last month's rent. You can argue until you're blue in the face. But the savvy tenant knows that it will take you more than a month to evict him or her and cost you a lot more than the security deposit. So in the end, if they use it as the last month's rent, there's not a whole lot you can do.

Usually most tenant's are not that savvy (unless they've read this book). However, even those who are and who do tell you to use the cleaning/security deposit as the last month's rent will often leave the property respectably clean. The reason is that they don't want to get you too mad. If they leave the property dirty, you could always turn around and sue them in small claims court for the lost rent and the damage they did over the amount covered by the deposit.

Some states are now requiring landlords, even landlords of single-family residences, to keep security/cleaning deposits in a separate account and to pay the tenant interest on it. Check with a good property management firm in your state. Also, you may still use a "lease" form without getting the last month's rent.

TRAP

Getting the first month's rent plus a security deposit does not necessarily mean you are limited to month-to-month tenancy.

Key #7—Rent for Less

It's important not to be penny wise and pound foolish when you rent. The foolish landlord tries to get top dollar for a property. The wise landlord rents for just below the market.

The reasoning is simple: To get top dollar you have to wait for a tenant. If you rent just below the market, your property will always be full.

But, some newcomers to renting may ask, "Aren't you losing money that way?"

Consider: You're renting a house where the market for a property such as yours is $1100 a month. So you put your property up for $1070. You'll lose $30 a month because you're renting below market. At the end of a year it will mean a loss of $360.

On the other hand, you'll rent up immediately. All else being equal, tenants will choose your property first over similar properties renting at $1100. Your property will be full all the time. (It's the same as when you go into the supermarket and see two products of equal quality next to each other. Don't you buy the one that's five cents less than the other, even though the price difference is negligible? Tenants act the same way.)

Now consider the landlord who insists on $1100 a month. Assuming that the market value is correct, he or she will get it. But, it might take a month until a tenant is found. This will result in a loss of $1100 of potential rent during that month. Is it better to lose $360 or $1100?

But some readers may ask, you'll keep losing money year after year. After awhile the other landlord has a better deal because he's charging more.

Not at all. At the end of the year, if you have a strong tenant who wants to stay, raise your rent to the market level. If it's still $1100, raise it to that point. The tenant shouldn't want to move because, after all, you've just adjusted the rent to the true market value. Besides, moving is a terrible hassle, and no one wants to do it for a savings of $30 a month.

On the other hand, your competitor who started at the higher price can't raise rents because he or she would then be above the market.

What we're talking about here is the rent-up period. You want to get your property rented fast because every day it's vacant costs you money. Renting just below the market will accomplish this.

Key #8—Charge
for Late Rent

This sometimes works for tenants who are always late. In any event, it's a good idea to include it in every rental agreement you write.

The penalty typically takes this form: In the rental agreement you include a clause that has words to the effect if that tenant does not get the rent in by a certain number of days after the due date (typically five days' grace is given), there is a penalty. The penalty is usually $50 or 5 percent of the rent, whichever is smaller.

This rent penalty is no more enforceable than the overall rental contract (meaning that you have to go to court to get enforcement, which you would most likely not do over $50). Nevertheless, in this modern world we are all conditioned to watch out for money penalties, and tenants are no different. You'd be surprised how careful they will be to get the rent in on time to avoid the penalty.

One caution: You have to enforce the clause. If the rent is late and does not contain the $50, you may want to refuse to accept the rent until the $50 is paid. This runs the small risk of not getting any rent. On the other hand, having once paid a penalty for late rent, the tenant probably will pay on time ever after.

A version of this works well with tenants who are already in the premises but do not have such a clause in their lease and begin paying later and later each month. This is the rent discount. What you do is raise the rent for this tenant. Very carefully you explain that it's been so long since you've raised the rent, that your costs have gone up, and so forth, and, in conclusion, you feel that a $50 a month rent increase is warranted, to take effect immediately (or upon termination of the current lease).

However, if the tenant gets the rent in on time, there will be a $50 discount. In other words, the rent may be $1050. However, if the rent is delivered on time, it is reduced to $1000. You'll be surprised at how many tenants will work hard to get that rent in when due.

Key #9—Don't Delay in Fixing a Problem

When you become a landlord you also assume the duties of a "fix-it person." You are expected to take care of all the little, as well as the big, things that go wrong. This includes fixing leaky toilets and plugged drains, sprinkler systems that don't turn on, and light switches that don't turn off. What's more, you're expected to fix these things quickly!

Although you might put up with a leaky toilet for weeks, a tenant who feels he or she is paying big bucks for the property won't put up with it at all. When they want things fixed, they want them fixed yesterday. If you don't respond and at least make the attempt to promptly correct the situation, you could lose your tenant.

Most states allow tenants to correct defective situations themselves and then deduct the cost from the rent up to certain limits. This is a definite "no-no" as far as you are concerned. The tenant might hire a plumber to fix a faucet and it would cost you $100, while you could have fixed it yourself for the cost of a washer.

If you can't fix things yourself, get the services of a handyman who can. Rest assured there will always be something to fix, and it's important to fix it fast.

Key #10—Keep an Eye on Your Property

A rental property is a valuable asset. You may have hundreds of thousands of dollars invested in it. You've given it up to someone to live in for several hundreds of dollars month. But that doesn't mean they are going to look after that asset as you would. Therefore, check up on your property.

TIP

Don't wait until the tenant doesn't pay. Check up at least once a month, even if it's just to drive by.

Of course, you don't want to make a pest of yourself. Your rental agreement should give you the right to inspect the inside of the house with reasonable notice. But don't always be bothering a tenant who's paying the rent and keeping the place in good shape. As noted, just driving by once and a while can be enough.

When you see those lawns start turning brown and the flowers in front drying up, you know you've got a problem. Stop by and check it out. It's better to find out earlier than later that your tenant lost his or her job Maybe you can help this tenant find another job or, at the least, another, lower-cost rental.

Don't let things slip. You're the one who will get hurt in the long run.

Key #11—Don't Let the Tenant Get Behind

What can you do when the payments are late and the penalty doesn't work?

This is another judgment call. Definitely speak to the tenant. Find out what the problem is. Maybe the tenant is waiting for a check to come in. If the late payment happens infrequently and there's a good reason, perhaps it's best to overlook it.

But what if the tenant is very late—one or two weeks late?

Remember, your cleaning/security deposit is typically only equal to one month's rent. If the tenant is two weeks late, he or she has already used up half the security deposit. Another two weeks and it's gone. Plus, if you have to evict, there's another month or two lost.

TRAP

Most savvy landlords don't accept any late rent at all.

If the rent is more than a day or two late, call or check with the tenant to see what the problem is. With a good tenant, it's usually an oversight, and after that the rent's right on time. With a bad tenant, it's excuses.

If the rent's more than a week late without sufficient explanation, savvy landlords send an official notice.

This can take various forms. Usually it's a three- or four-day notice telling the tenant to pay or quit. The time length is determined by each state. It is normally the first step required in an eviction. You can pick up the form at any stationary store or from an attorney's office. And tenants, particularly those who are regular late payers, know it.

One such notice is usually sufficient to convince a tenant that you mean business.

If the tenant still refuses to pay after two weeks, most savvy landlords begin eviction (discussed next). Note: Waiting two weeks really doesn't cost you anything since most courts won't consider an unlawful detainer action until the tenant is at least two weeks late in rent and has used up the security/cleaning deposit.

The above time limits, however, are not set in stone. As with most things in renting property, it's a judgment call. On the one hand, you don't want to scare, embarrass, or anger a good tenant into leaving just because one month they happened to overlook the rental due date. On the other hand, you don't want to give a bad tenant any more time than is absolutely necessary.

As I said, there is no one set answer. You have to play each case on its own merits. For myself, however, I would never let a tenant go more than two weeks without paying the rent no matter what the situation or how good I thought the tenant was. There's just too much at stake for me to lose.

Key #12—Evict Only as a Last Resort

Finally, you may at some time in your career as a landlord need to evict a tenant who won't pay the rent and who won't quit the premises.

Remember that self-help evictions in which you physically throw the tenants out onto the street are no longer allowed in virtually any area. Now you must go to court to get a tenant out and, if it's the first or even second time you do this, you'll need the help of an eviction attorney.

Don't call just any attorney. Check around with local brokers, particularly those who handle property management. Usually there are one or two attorneys in town who do nothing but handle evictions. Call one. This attorney undoubtedly already has set fees and knows the ropes. He or she can get the tenant out with a minimum amount of cost and time to you.

In addition, be sure that the attorney gets a judgment against the tenant for back rent owed. Often the attorney, or his or her investigators, can follow the former tenant to a new location and a new job and garnish wages to recoup your back rent. Usually their costs and fees are not deducted from the rent owed you. You may eventually get back everything you are owed! (Don't count on that happening every time, however.)

By the way, just getting the unlawful detainer judgment and eviction notice isn't the end. To finally get the bad tenant out, you will probably have to pay the sheriff. The officers will come and will literally move the tenant out. (Usually even the worst tenants will voluntarily leave once they realize that the sheriff is coming.)

When a nonpaying tenant won't quit, be prepared for a loss. Chances are you'll lose some rent, at least the rent until the tenant is evicted. You'll probably also get the place back in a mess, so there will be cleanup costs. Note also that some tenants cannot be evicted! In some states a tenant who is in the last stages of pregnancy or is seriously ill and can provide a doctor's letter stating that he or she cannot be moved may be allowed to stay in the property at your expense. A tenant involved in bankruptcy may make the eviction proceedings part of the bankruptcy proceedings and postpone eviction. If you stay a landlord long enough, you'll see all kinds of problems.

The Bottom Line

The bottom line is that while all sorts of problems can happen, they rarely do. You may rent property all your life and never run into a quarter of the problems we've discussed in just this one chapter. On the other hand, you could be unlucky and get them all in the first year!

Most landlords are successful and go on to sell their properties later for hefty profits.

[Note: The previous keys first appeared as rules in Robert Irwin, *Buy, Rent, and Sell* (McGraw-Hill, 2001). For more information on landlording, check into my book *The Landlord's Trouble-Shooter*, 4th ed. (Dearborn, 2002).

11
Tricks of the Purchase Agreement

If you're going to be investing in real estate, there's one rule you need to understand and follow. Put simply, it's "Get everything in writing."

Indeed, according to the Statute of Frauds, most real estate transactions must be in writing to be enforced. An agent normally can't force you to pay a commission unless you've agreed to it in writing. And you can't force a seller to go through with a sale unless you have it in writing.

The most important document, therefore, usually becomes the purchase agreement (also called the *deposit receipt* and *sales agreement*). It should specify not only the price you'll pay for a property, but also the terms of the purchase down to the finest detail. All of which is to say that while some of the negotiations may actually take place verbally, it's what's on paper that ultimately counts.

Simple, you may be thinking. I'll just be sure everything we agree upon is written down.

Not so simple. Sometimes your interpretation of the purchase agreement may differ from that of the other party. Other times, you may think a point is agreed upon in a certain way, only to discover that it's different because of precedent or tradition.

In short, the purchase agreement can be a very tricky document. Depending on how it's written, it can advance your position, or cost you serious money. In this chapter we're going to consider a few of its trickier turning points.

TRAP

Before signing any purchase agreement, you should have your agent and attorney thoroughly check it over. It's intended to be a legally binding agreement and often represents hundreds of thousands of dollars. With that much money at stake, you don't want to take any chances.

How Much Money Should I Risk?

Almost all purchase agreements should be accompanied by a deposit. The deposit is money that you put up at the time you make an offer on a piece of property to show that you are in earnest about buying it. Hence the deposit is actually *earnest money*. An offer can be made without a deposit. However, a seller is less likely to accept it. After all, without a deposit you have very little to lose by not following through on the deal.

Some investors feel it's important to put up a big deposit. They feel that this will help convince the seller to accept the offer. While this might have been the case years ago, it's no longer true. The reason is that a modern purchase agreement is filled with contingencies that make the document as loose as a sponge, at least initially.

For example, the deal is rarely solid until you've approved a professional inspection and the seller's disclosures and until you've locked in financing. If these contingencies aren't removed, the deal doesn't go forward, and your deposit is normally returned. Thus, since it's not really at that much risk in the initial stages of a transaction, a large deposit today won't impress the seller's agent. And it won't impress a sharp seller.

On the other hand, it's your money that's tied up. And no matter how likely it is that it will be returned, there's always the chance that something might go sour and you could lose it—hence, there is a risk for you. Therefore, it's often to your advantage to put up only a token deposit, at least initially.

I say initially because if you really want to impress a seller with your sincerity in buying the property, you can agree to increase your deposit substantially, once the contingencies (see below) have been removed. Increasing the deposit assures the seller that you are in earnest about completing the transaction and can sometimes mean the difference between getting a seller to agree to a deal or not.

Keep in mind, of course, that your deposit is very much at risk once contingencies have been removed. Increasing it at that time only increases your exposure. (Which, of course, is the very reason it impresses sellers.) You won't want to increase your deposit unless and until you're sure you're going to go through with the purchase.

TIP

A deposit doesn't necessarily have to be in the form of cash. It can be a promissory note or a check that all parties agree not to cash, or even personal property, such as the title to a car or boat. Cash (cashier's check), however, talks the loudest when you're trying to convince a seller to accept an offer.

Sometimes sellers will specify in a listing agreement that they will accept no offers with less than, for example, a $10,000 cash deposit. Remember, however, everything is negotiable. You can always offer a smaller deposit and in a different form. However, if the seller is demanding a cash deposit, the agent may not be required to submit lesser offers, depending on how the listing agreement was signed.

Most agents, however, will submit any and all offers.

What If the Deal Doesn't Go Through?

Don't assume that just because you and the seller have signed a purchase agreement it's a done deal. Actually, the purchase agreement is only the beginning of the transaction. It usually ends a month or so later when escrow closes. In between, a host of problems can occur to nix the deal.

When it's through no fault of yours that the deal doesn't go through, you can reasonably expect to get your deposit back. However, don't assume that this will automatically happen. There can be delays and difficulties at best. And sometimes, depending on

how things turn out, you could stand to lose some or all of the
money you put up.

TRAP

Losing the deposit is not necessarily the worst that can
happen. If it is your fault that the deal falls through,
the seller can take you to court and sue for "specific
performance," demanding that you continue with the
purchase and/or damages.

In most cases, however, there's enough blame to go around on all
sides when a deal falls through. And if you have a contingency to rely
upon (you couldn't get financing, you disapprove the seller's disclosures, or the professional inspection), you are likely to get your
deposit back.

Should You Give the Deposit to the Seller?

The seller is entitled to the deposit. However, the seller is the last person in the world you want to give the deposit to. The seller might
immediately spend the money then later on, if the deal falls through,
not be able to refund it to you, even if you're entitled to get it back.
It could require the services of an attorney and a lawsuit to secure the
return of the deposit from the seller, and that could be very costly. In
other words, giving the deposit to the seller could be like dropping it
down a deep hole.

You want the deposit to go to a neutral party who will not frivolously
spend the money, but who will hold it and have it on hand to pay you
back, if necessary. The first most likely candidate here is the agent.

TIP

Real estate agents are required to maintain trust accounts
for any money they receive. In other words, they aren't
supposed to commingle (mix) your money with their
own, but must hold it in a separate account in trust for
you. This is to keep them from spending your money.

Although an agent's fiduciary account sounds safe, the problem is that, in theory, the deposit belongs to the seller and, if the seller demands it, the seller's agent is supposed to hand the deposit over. Most agents, however, are as wary of the seller as you are and will do everything possible to hold the money in trust until the deal closes.

To ensure that they don't lose their licenses, agents will almost always bend over backward to repay any money stuck in their trust accounts. Further, many states have special recovery funds. If you lose money through the carelessness (or fraud) of an agent, you may be able to recover it from the state, even though it could take years. Check with your state's department of real estate.

Today, many good agents realize that accepting a check for a deposit puts them at great risk. If the deal doesn't go through, both the buyer and the seller may demand the money, leaving the agent in the middle. To avoid this, many agents suggest you write the deposit check out to an escrow company which, you agree in advance, will handle the escrow of the property if and when the seller accepts. In other words, give the deposit to a neutral party. Sound good?

There is also peril here. If, after the seller accepts, the deal still falls apart, even through no fault of your own, it might be hard to get the deposit back from even a neutral escrow.

The reason is that escrows simply handle the documents and funds in a transaction. In order for an escrow to operate, both buyer *and* seller must agree to the escrow's instructions. If, for example, you tell the escrow to return your money and the seller tells the escrow to hold onto it, there's no agreement. And your money remains in limbo. This affects you more than the seller. After all, it's your money.

Sometimes, in this situation sellers are content to let the money sit in an inactive escrow for months just to "punish" a buyer for a deal that falls through. Fortunately, calmer minds usually prevail, and sellers eventually will agree to release your funds once they become convinced that there's no way they can get the money and that to continue to hold it might result in a lawsuit against them.

What must be obvious by now is that putting up a deposit is some-times a tricky thing. Operating on the principle that the time to con-sult an attorney is before you need one, I once again advise you to seek the services of a professional real estate lawyer before signing the purchase agreement. Chances are you're going to need one anyway before the deal is concluded, and by bringing the lawyer in at an early stage, you could avoid much grief.

What If the Deal Falls Through Because of the Seller?

When the seller defaults, you usually will get the deposit back. Often the seller is more than happy to do everything to get that deposit back to you in the hope that you won't take further action.

However, you may still want the property. And if the seller doesn't have grounds for getting out of the deal, you may be able to sue him or her for specific performance (going through with the sale), and/or damages. Check with your attorney to see what further action, if any, you should take.

What If It's No One's Fault?

There are a lot of reasons that a deal might not go through. You may not be able to secure adequate financing. The title to the property may not be clear. There could be extensive termite damage. It could turn out that the house is in the middle of a flood plain. The reasons are endless, and they crop up in a good many deals.

In most cases there's a way to work them out. Other financing is secured. The seller clears the title. The termite damage is fixed. You agree to accept the risk of flood damage for a lower price (and by securing adequate insurance), and so on. In other words, the problems are solved one way or another.

However, sometimes it just doesn't work, and there's no deal to be made. What happens to your deposit then?

If you've given it to an agent who has kept it in a personal trust account, you can demand it back, and in most cases the agent will, indeed, return it (perhaps risking the ire of the seller). If the conditions of the purchase agreement can't be fulfilled, normally you're entitled to get it back, and most agents don't want to argue the point.

On the other hand, if the deposit's been placed in an escrow account, it normally takes both buyer's and seller's agreement to get it out.

Maybe the seller is angry that the deal fell through and says, "I'm not signing anything." There your deposit sits, even though you're perfectly entitled to it. Unless the agent can prevail and convince the seller to release it, it could remain there for a long time!

As a practical matter, however, as soon as another buyer comes along, the seller probably will be forced to release it so as not to jeopardize a later sale.

What If the Seller Doesn't Accept My Offer or Counters the Offer?

That's easy, or should be. If the seller does not accept your offer, there's no deal, and you're entitled to your deposit back immediately. It's just that simple.

The seller has to agree to your entire offer, including any terms you propose. If the seller agrees to the price but not the terms and counters with different terms that you don't accept, there's no deal, and you're entitled to your money back. If the seller accepts your terms but counters with a different price that you don't accept, the deal's off, and you're entitled to your deposit back.

TIP

The moment the seller declines your offer and *counters* (proposes a deal different in some way, no matter how small), the original offer is normally considered dead. Unless you accept the seller's counteroffer, you're entitled to your deposit back.

Can I Protect Myself with a "Liquidated Damages" Clause?

Basically, *liquidated damages clauses* state that if you and the seller agree in advance, the deposit (or a portion of it) will constitute the entire damages the seller is entitled to in the event of your default. In other words, if the deal doesn't go through and it's clearly your fault, you agree in advance that the seller can keep the deposit, provided she or he agrees not to sue you for additional damages or specific performance.

Some investors use this clause to tie up a property that they are unsure about. They sign a contract offering a small deposit, say $1000, and insist that the seller sign the liquidated damages clause. Afterward, if they decide not to purchase and back out, they hope that the only penalty they'll have to pay is the $1000 and that, because of the clause, the seller can't come back at them for anything more.

This may or may not work. Sometimes a clever attorney can break the liquidated damages clause, perhaps by showing that your intention never was to purchase the property.

When it comes to liquidated damage clauses, ask your attorney. On the one hand, signing the clause (assuming the seller also signs) helps to limit your loss to the deposit. On the other hand, it may insure that you'll lose the entire deposit; whereas, depending on the situation, you might otherwise get back at least a portion of it.

Escape Clauses

As an investor you will certainly want to be sure that any purchase agreement you sign has escape clauses. These are contingencies built into the contract that allow you to gracefully back out of the deal without problems (and let you get your deposit back).

You'll want escape clauses for two reasons. The first is the same reason that any buyer wants them, to protect yourself. You'll want to be sure you aren't committed to go through with the deal if you can't get financing or if the house proves to have lots of defects.

The second reason is that investors typically want to keep their options open. Yes, you've agreed to purchase. But what if a better deal comes along? Is there someway out so you can take advantage of it? Technically speaking, escape clauses should not be used for this purpose. But practically speaking, investors use them as such all the time. So let's see how they work.

What Is an Escape Clause?

An *escape clause* is essentially any contingency written into a contract that says the offer depends or hinges on some other event or action.

For example, wording that would say "This offer is contingent upon the buyer's inheriting money from her uncle" is a kind of contingency clause.

I once knew an investor whose advice was, "Never sign a purchase agreement unless it has escape clauses in it." Be sure they say "subject to . . . ."

The words *subject to* have essentially the same meaning as *contingent*. They make the sales offer hinge on some event or action. What my investor friend meant was that so long as those words were in it, he felt he could get out of the contract if he had to.

Some contingencies are absolutely necessary for the sales agreement, and few agents would hesitate to put them in. Typical contingency clauses include those that follow.

Typical Escape Clauses

- **Seller's Disclosures**—You have the right to approve the seller's property disclosures. Don't approve them and there's no deal.

- **Your Professional Inspection**—You have the right to approve a professional inspection report. Don't approve it and the deal's off.

- **New Financing**—If you can't get the financing you need, there is no deal and you get your deposit back.

Investors, however, may want additional contingencies. For example, you may want a clause that says the deal is subject to your getting approval for a zoning change. You may have it in mind to develop the property by turning a home into, for example, a child-care center, and you can only do it if the zoning commission agrees.

Or, you may want a contingency that lets you out of the deal if you can't refinance a different property, one from which you plan to take the money to buy the current one. A typical escape clause that both investors and home buyers often insist on is that the purchase is subject to the sale of their current houses. If their current houses don't sell, they're out of the deal.

The Big Problem with Escape Clauses

The more escape clauses you put into a contract, the more protection you have for yourself. Unfortunately, the less protection the other party has. As a consequence, if as a buyer you load up the contract with escape clauses, you diminish your chances that the seller will agree to sell.

Similarly, sellers will sometimes insist on lots of escape clauses in a purchase agreement. If they do, you may be wise to ditch the deal.

TIP

The rule is that although escape clauses offer protection, they weaken your offer. Try to include as few as possible, while at the same time maintaining those you absolutely need to protect yourself.

By the way, be sure your contingency is written properly. The wrong wording may not protect you. Some purchase agreements have the most common contingencies already written in. Your agent simply checks the appropriate box, and the contingency is in effect. Of course, you may want to have your attorney check the language used in the agreement.

If a new contingency is to be written, it should handled by an attorney. This does not mean that a good agent can't do it. Many agents with years of experience can handle these easily. Even so, it wouldn't hurt to have an attorney recheck it, just to be sure.

Take Charge of Time

Many real estate contracts include the phrase that "time is of the essence." It essentially means that everything must be done in a timely fashion, as specified. If deadlines are not met, there may be penalties, the deal may be lost, and the deposit may be forfeited. As an investor, you should make sure you understand the time conditions of your purchase agreement and make every effort to control them so they are doable and, if possible, favorable.

As with everything in real estate, time is negotiable. How long do you have to secure financing, to come up with the down payment and closing costs, to close the escrow, to take possession and move in?

For example, you're buying a house, and the seller has children who are enrolled in a local school. It's April and school isn't out until early June. Therefore, the seller wants enough time for the kids to finish school before moving out. In this case it's probably 90 days.

But you figure that you can easily get financing and close the deal in 30 days. There's a time difference of 60 days.

Sure, you can be a nice person and simply agree to give the seller the additional 60 days. Or, you can be a hard-boiled businessperson and insist on something in return for your concession on time. Perhaps you'll want a small drop in price. Maybe you'll insist the sellers leave that refrigerator. Certainly you'll insist that if the deal closes before the sellers move out, they execute a strict rental agreement and include a hefty security deposit. (Renting back to sellers is always tricky because if they later can't or won't move, they have tenant's rights, and you may need to go through an eviction, along with its costs and delays, to get them out.)

Remember that time is an important element of every purchase agreement. Use it wisely, and it will help you get a better deal.

Can I Get Out of the Deal on the Final Walk-Through?

Most buyers insist on a clause in the purchase agreement that gives them the right to a final walk-through inspection before the deal closes. If the property isn't in the same condition as it was when the offer was made, the buyer can demand it be brought back to its previous condition. In very severe cases, if, for example, a fire burned down a portion of the home, the buyer may be able to get out of the deal.

The final walk-through is not supposed to be an opportunity for you to back out of the deal. It is just supposed to be a chance for you to examine the property and make sure that it's as it was when you originally made your offer. Most savvy sellers will include a clause stating that if something of consequence is found wrong, the sellers have the right to correct it—that the final walk-through is not intended to be a new beginning in negotiating price or terms.

Nevertheless, savvy investors have used faults found on final inspections to back out of deals at the last minute. (Their reasons can vary from finding a serious fault in the property to finding another, more preferable house.) My suggestion is that if you want to renegotiate based on the final walk-though, you had better have found some serious problem with the house, or else you'll have an angry seller to contend with.

By the way, expect dirt and minor damage to be present on your final walk-through. After the sellers move their furniture and carpeting, small defects are always present and are to be expected.

TIP

Insist that the utilities be on when you check out the property. Otherwise, you won't be able to tell if any of the house's systems are broken.

Should I Rely on a Professional Home Inspection?

Yes and no.

Inspectors are increasingly getting better, and many states have started licensing them. Nevertheless, as an investor you'll want to develop your own techniques for evaluating the condition of a property.

By all means have it professionally inspected. But then, be sure to check it out yourself. And have any professionals in the field whom you know (plumber, electrician, carpenter, heat/cooling contractor, roofer, and so on) check it out as well.

Should an Investor Insist on a Home Protection Plan?

Absolutely. Several national and some local companies offer plans that give you insurance protection for the major systems of the home. Typically they cover plumbing (including water heater), heating, air conditioning, electrical, appliances, and so forth. The idea is that for a set period of time after you buy (typically one year), if there should be a problem, the home protection company will cover it. The cost is usually nominal, a few hundred dollars for a year's worth of coverage.

In most purchases the sellers pay for the plan; you pay the deductible (usually under $50) for each time you call someone out to deal with a problem. Most plans are renewable, so if you like the one you've got, you can keep it. (Of course, you'll have to pay for it after the first year.)

Whether you plan to move in or rent out the home, the protection plan is highly desirable. After all, you never know what can go wrong in the first year after you make a purchase. And the plan can save you considerable amounts of money. Besides, it's usually an added bonus since most often it's the seller who pays for it.

Should I Agree to an Arbitration Clause?

Some sales agreements contain arbitration clauses. These may refer only to the deposit, or they may refer to the entire purchase agreement. Basically what they say is that if there is a disagreement, you will submit it to binding arbitration—you will go along with whatever an arbitrator says.

Keep in mind that you could be giving up significant rights if you sign an arbitration agreement. If the seller refuses to go through with the deal after you've made all sorts of commitments, you might want the right to sue for damages.

You could lose the option of suing the seller for damages or specific performance (forcing them to sell to you) by signing this clause. On the other hand, the sellers could be giving up the same rights, meaning that you could be avoiding the risk of being sued. If you agree to arbitration, just remember that for it to be effective both you (the buyer) and the seller have to agree. If just one agrees, it won't work.

Also, be sure you know who the arbitrator will be. Many arbitration clauses specify that the arbitrator will be a member of the American Arbitration Association (local members are listed in the yellow pages of your phone book). This is fine, since such members are skilled at arbitration. But they are also quite expensive. It really doesn't make much sense to use an arbitrator when his or her fee may exceed the worth of the item being arbitrated.

It's a good idea to ask your attorney about this clause.

Watch Out for the Purchase Agreement

The purchase agreement is where you make your deal (good, bad, or mediocre) and define how the purchase process will be followed until the house is yours. Take time with it, make sure that you understand it thoroughly, and be sure that it gives you all the protection you can get.

TRAP

Don't sign any purchase agreement until you've had it explained to you by your agent and until your attorney has had an opportunity to check it over. Remember, when you sign, your signature is your bond. Be sure you're making the best deal possible.

Be Wary of Overly Zealous Attorneys

Beware of attorneys who work too hard for your interests. In general, real estate agents dread attorneys, not because they don't protect people, but because they tend to muck up deals. There's an old saying among real estate agents that the fastest way to have a deal go sour is to bring in an attorney. Yes, you want your rights protected, and you want the most favorable terms. But you also want to be able ultimately to purchase the property. An attorney can create a sales contract so favorable to you that no seller will accept it. As with the ancient Greeks, moderation is in order. Allow your attorney to draw up the terms correctly and to advise. But also rely on common sense.

12

Working the Tax Laws to Your Advantage

Special Note

The author is not engaged in providing tax advice. The following is simply an overview of tax rules generally affecting real estate investment property. However, tax rules and their application frequently change. You should not rely on the material in this chapter. For tax advice specific to your situation and property(s), consult with a tax professional.

When you invest in real estate you'll either make a profit or show a loss. (You'll seldom exactly break even.) Either way, there are legal tax rules that can help you out if you know what they are and take advantage of them.

I'm not talking here about hidden loopholes. Rather, these are the tax rules that all investors must follow. It's just a matter of designing your real estate investments to take advantage of them.

What If I Make a Profit?

Making a profit, of course, is the goal. If you've held the property for more than a year, you'll probably owe capital gains tax on it. (We'll see how to make the calculations later in this chapter.) Currently the capital gains tax rate is 15 percent for most investors—not terrible,

147

but still substantial. On a $500,000 profit, that means that you would pay roughly $100,000 in capital gains taxes.

Can this tax be avoided legally?

Perhaps. One method that might be used is to convert the property from an investment to a personal residence (assuming it isn't already such). You can remove the tenants and move in yourself, declaring the property your principal residence. After living in the property for a period of time (you must reside in the property for two out of the previous five years), you may then be able to sell the home and reap the benefits of the principal residence capital gains exclusion of up to $500,000 per couple filing jointly (up to $250,000 for individuals).

TIP

In real estate you only owe capital gains taxes when you sell. No matter how high the value of your property goes, you don't pay tax on the gain so long as you continue to own it. (You would, of course, owe income taxes if you showed excess income over expenses on an annual basis, and you would also owe property taxes.)

Under the 1997 Taxpayer Relief Act, each person, regardless of age, can exclude up to $250,000 of the capital gain on a principle residence. For a couple filing jointly, that multiplies to $500,000.

Note that the exclusion can only be taken on a principal residence. It *cannot* be taken on investment property, unless that investment property was previously converted to a principle residence. There are some fine-print rules involved in the exclusion that your professional tax adviser can explain to you, but the big rule to keep in mind is that, in order to obtain the exclusion, you must have lived in the property for two of the previous five years.

TIP

You owe tax on a capital gain regardless of whether the property is investment or personal residence. However, if you sell at a capital loss, you can take a deduction against that loss if it's on investment property but you can't take a deduction against that loss if it's on a personal residence! A quirk in the tax laws.

That means two things. First, you've got to live in the property (not just own it) for 2 years before you can claim the exclusion. Second, you can only do this once every 2 years. Thus, if you own 15 properties, it would take you 30 years at minimum to take the exclusion on all of them in this fashion!

An additional problem has to do with any depreciation taken while you owned the property. The rules seem to change frequently, but you might find that the depreciation is recaptured. Thus, even though you may avoid paying taxes on some of your capital gain by using the personal property exclusion, you might still owe some taxes on the recaptured depreciation losses that you took earlier.

What about Trading?

Trading may offer a method of legally deferring the tax you would otherwise pay on a sale. You can trade or exchange your investment property for another and defer the capital gain from the old property to the new. This is technically called a Section 1031(a)(3) tax deferred exchange.

A great many investors see this as a means of multiplying their profits without paying taxes along the way. They hopscotch from property to property, increasing the value of their real estate holdings unencumbered by paying taxes on the gain for each transaction.

The rules for a tax-free exchange were greatly simplified over a decade ago by several tax cases, the most famous of which resulted in what is called the *Starker Rule*. Under Starker, you just go ahead and sell your investment property as you would otherwise. However, you have 45 days before or after the sale to designate a new property into which you will invest your money. And you have 180 days to close the deal on that new property. (You can designate an arm's length entity—one that you cannot touch—such as a title insurance company escrow account to hold your money from the sale until it's ready to go into the new property.)

TRAP

There are other strict conditions of the exchange that must be met. One is that you may not take cash out (boot out) as part of the sale. If you want cash out, you must usually refinance either the old property before the exchange or the new property after it.

Another condition is that only like-kind properties can be exchanged. This means that the property must be held for business or investment. It does not mean that you can only exchange, for example, an apartment building for another apartment building. Any real estate held for investment (house, apartment building, lot) might be exchanged for another.

TRAP

Tax-deferred exchanges are a tricky business. Do not attempt one until you've contacted both an agent and an accountant/attorney familiar with how they are done for assistance.

Can I Combine an Exchange and a Personal Property Exclusion?

One of the problems we noted earlier with converting an investment property into a personal property is that you may not want to reside in a property you own as an investment. If that's the case, then there may be another answer. You could do a tax-deferred exchange of the investment property into one in which you would like to live. Then convert the home you desire to live in from investment to principal residence.

Keep in mind, however, the like-kind rule noted above. A personal residence is not the same as an investment house.

TRAP

A personal residence is not a property held for investment and, presumably, would not meet the like-kind rule.

Therefore, in order to avoid invalidating the tax-deferred status of the exchange, you might have to rent out the new property as an investment for a time before moving in yourself. How long must you wait before converting it to a principal residence? Some tax advisers have suggested six months, others as long as two years or more. Again, check with your own professional tax adviser.

Understanding Depreciation

If you own investment real estate, you can depreciate it. Depreciating means taking a certain percentage of its "cost" (we'll talk more about this later) each year as a reduction in value.

Almost all business assets can be depreciated. Apartment furniture and refrigerators, for example, are depreciated over a lifespan of five years. In a straight-line method, you might take 20 percent of the cost as a loss of value per year.

Residential rental real estate must be depreciated over 27.5 years. Again, using a straight-line method you would take 1/27.5 of the cost each year as a loss in value.

Of course, the value of property goes up, not down. So, how you can take a loss on an asset that's increasing in value? A helpful way to understand this is to think of it is as a "paper loss." All assets deteriorate over time. Even a house will eventually fall away to dust. So instead of simply waiting until the end of its useful lifespan (arbitrarily decided by the government), you take a portion of the loss in value each year.

The time span of 27.5 years is specified by the government, and it is quite arbitrary. In the past, much shorter time spans have been allowed. But, you may reasonably wonder, although the house will eventually deteriorate, the land never will. How do you depreciate land costs?

TIP

You can only depreciate a building, not the land it sits on.

You can't depreciate land. The only exceptions would be if the land itself had an asset that was depletable, such as gas and oil, and that's not the case here. Depreciation is an expense much in the way you have other expenses when you own rental property. For example, here's a list of some expenses you might expect to incur:

Typical Rental Property Expenses

- Mortgage interest
- Taxes
- Insurance
- Water service
- Garbage service
- Maintenance and repair
- Fix-up
- Advertising
- Pool and gardener service
- Depreciation

When you add up all of these expenses, you have the total expenses for your property over a month. Add all the monthlies together, and that's how much it costs you over a year.

Now, subtract your total annual expenses from your total annual income, and that's your profit or loss.

Depreciation goes on the expense side and, as such, can increase your loss. As soon as you begin to look at properties out there in the real world, you'll come to realize that finding one where the income comes even close to paying for the actual cash expenses is rare. When you add the paper loss of depreciation to your cash expenses, you almost always find that there's a loss.

Typical Income/Expense on a Rental House

Total annual income	$14,440 ($1200 monthly)
Total annual cash expenses	−14,000 (without depreciation)
Positive cash flow	440
Annual depreciation	−7500
Annual loss	−7060

Once depreciation is added in, you can almost always be assured that any property recently acquired for little or nothing down will show a loss, at least on paper. In our above example, a good property that actually shows a positive cash flow (more money coming in than cash expenses going out) turns into a big loser as soon as depreciation is added. Remember that the loss from depreciation is not an out-of-pocket expense. It's simply an accounting loss. It only shows up on paper.

In the dim past, depreciation was a tax dodge that was used by the wealthy to reduce their sizeable incomes. They would take the loss from real estate (that only occurred on paper) and deduct it from their ordinary income. That reduced their ordinary income and, of course, reduced the amount of taxes they would owe on that income. Later, when they sold, they would pay a lower capital gains tax. Converting the tax from ordinary income to capital gains was the dodge.

That tax shelter was largely eliminated for the wealthy by the Tax Reform Act of 1986. Now it is only available if your income is less than $150,000. We'll have more to say about this shortly.

The Benefits of Depreciation

Let's go back to when we were earlier saying that depreciation reduced the "cost" of the building by a certain amount each year. Although the cost is the most common method of establishing a tax basis, it's not the only consideration.

For tax purposes there is a *basis* to each asset. That is the amount used for making tax calculations such as depreciation or, when you sell, for capital gains.

TIP

Depreciation reduces the tax basis of the property.

The basis for most assets, as we said, is their cost. However, with homes that basis can vary. For example, there are substantial transaction fees when you buy a home. Most of these are added to the basis.

Or, you may build an addition to the home. This is also added to the basis.

On the other hand, the basis may be reduced. Depreciation reduces the basis of the property. Here's how it works:

Change in Basis Due to Depreciation

Original basis (cost)	$200,000
Add a room	+ 30,000
Adjusted basis	230,000
Depreciation ($7000 annually for 10 years)	−70,000
New adjusted basis	160,000

Notice that although the property began with a basis of $200,000, which was its cost, that basis went up when a room was added and, more importantly here, went down when depreciation was calculated.

Mind Your Tax Basis

The reason that we've spent some time explaining basis is because it (and the sales price) determines the capital gains (and tax) you'll have to pay when you sell.

Your capital gain on the property is the difference between the adjusted tax basis and the sales price (including the costs of sale).

Calculating Capital Gain

Sales price (adjusted for costs of sale such as commission)	$300,000
Adjusted tax basis	160,000
Capital gain (on which tax is due)	140,000

Thus, to go through our example, you buy the property for $200,000, add a room for $30,000, which raises your basis, and then depreciate it for $70,000, which lowers the basis. When you sell, both the raising and lowering of the tax basis affects how big a capital gain you have. (Note: In some cases of accelerated depreciation, the amount depreciated is recaptured at ordinary income rates, not capital gains rates.)

All of which is to say that although depreciating real estate can produce a tax write-off, as noted earlier, when you sell, that tax loss all comes back to haunt you as a capital gain.

Thus, in decades past when anyone regardless of income could write off losses on real estate, what they were actually doing was converting their ordinary income to capital gains. Instead of paying high ordinary income taxes, they converted that income to a capital gain and paid lower capital gains taxes.

TIP

The great tax shelter benefit of real estate in the past was that it converted ordinary income to capital gains and reduced the tax rate.

Doesn't That Work Now?

Not really, for two reasons. The first is that the Tax Reform Act of 1986 eliminated high-income investors from taking a deduction on their real estate losses. And the Taxpayer Relief Act of 1997 reduced the capital gains rate (and added a few more wrinkles, as we'll shortly see).

To begin, however, let's consider the rules with regard to taking a loss from real estate as a deduction against your ordinary income.

Income from a Portfolio

This is income from dividends, interest, royalties, and anything similar. We need not worry much about this here except to note that it does not include real estate income.

Income That's "Active"

The tax law now distinguishes between the types of income that we receive. Income from wages or as compensation for services is called *active income*. It includes commissions, consulting fees, salary, or anything similar. It's important for those involved in real estate to note that profits and losses from businesses in which you "materially participate" are included. However, limited partnerships are not included. And especially, activities from real estate are specifically excluded.

Income That's "Passive"

This is a bit trickier to define, but in general it means the profit or loss that we receive from a business activity in which we do not materially participate. This includes not only limited partnerships but also income from any real estate that is rented out. It's important to note that real estate is specifically defined as passive.

Under the old law, income was income and loss was loss. You could, thus, deduct any loss on real estate from your other income. Under the current law your personal income is considered "active" while your real estate loss is considered "passive." Since you can't deduct a passive loss from active income, you can't, in general, write off any real estate losses.

We've already said that these rules were primarily aimed at the wealthy to eliminate a big tax shelter. But this advantage has been retained for the small investor.

There is an important exception to the above rule. This exception provides a $25,000 allowance for write-offs for those with lower ordinary income. In other words, you can write off up to $25,000 in losses from real estate against your active income, provided you meet an income ceiling (plus certain other qualifications).

Your Gross Adjusted Income Must Not Exceed $150,000

If your income is below $100,000, then you qualify for the entire $25,000 exception. If it is between $100,000 and $150,000, you lose 50 cents of the allowance for every dollar your income exceeds $100,000.

Since most small investors have incomes under $150,000 the allowance applies to them. They can deduct their losses on real estate up to the $25,000 limitation.

You Must Actively Participate in the Rental Process

You'll recall that we said there was another qualification. It is that you must actively participate in the business of renting the property.

This can be tricky. After all, what does "actively participate" really mean?

Obviously if you own the property and are the only person directly involved in handling the rental—you advertise it, rent it, handle maintenance and cleanup, collect the rent, etc.—then you materially participate.

However, there are gray zones. Generally, if you don't personally determine the rental terms, approve new tenants, sign for repairs, or approve capital improvements and the like, you may not qualify.

The question always comes up, "What if I hire a management firm to handle the property for me?"

This is even grayer. In general, a management firm is probably okay to use so long as you continue to materially participate (determine rental terms, approve new tenants, sign for repairs or capital improvements, and the like). If you are going to use a management firm, be sure that you have your attorney check over the agreement you sign with the firm to see that it does not characterize you as not materially participating and thus prevent you from deducting any loss.

TRAP

It may be difficult to prove that you participate materially in the running of your rental business. For example, you may need to show that you worked a minimum of 500 hours or more at it. Check with your tax professional for advice.

On the surface, the allowance and the qualifications may seem straightforward. But they can be tricky. For example, here are some other considerations:

1. The income used to determine whether you qualify is your gross adjusted income. This means your income after you have taken some deductions, such as retirement plan contributions (not IRAs), alimony, moving expenses, and others.

2. The allowance does not apply to farms. If you materially participate in the running of a farm, other rules apply. See your accountant or tax attorney.

3. Those who don't qualify for taking the deduction against their
   active income likewise cannot take the deduction against their
   portfolio income. (Remember, portfolio income came from
   interest, dividends, royalties, etc.)

TIP

When you sell, chances are you will owe some capital
gains, assuming you don't sell for a loss. However, as
noted, the capital gains tax rate has been reduced. At
the present time it's a maximum of 15 percent. Hence,
even if you do have to pay, it won't usually be a confis-
catory amount.

Keep All Your Receipts

From our discussion here, one other thing should be apparent: You
need good record keeping. It's very important that you keep every
receipt and note every expense and piece of income in a ledger.

You may have to prove to the IRS that expenses that you had on
your investment property were real. For example, three years earlier you had a vacancy, and you spent $115 in advertising to get a
new tenant.

Prove it, says the IRS. So, you reach into your bag of receipts and
pull out an invoice from the local paper for $115 for advertising.
Attached to it is a copy of the ad itself and your check in payment.
It's hard to dispute that.

Also, keep all records if you make improvements to the property.
Remember, improvements *raise* the tax basis, which will later reduce
the amount of capital gains you will need to pay. (The higher the tax
basis, the less the capital gain.)

If you make a capital improvement, such as put on a new room or
add a patio, keep all of the receipts. At the end of the year your
accountant will be able to use them to adjust your tax basis upward.

TIP

Just because you spend money improving your rental, doesn't mean that you've made a capital improvement for tax purposes. Replacing a water heater, for example, is not a capital improvement, it's a repair. Adding a tile roof where there was previously a less expensive tar roof probably would be a capital improvement (at least the difference in price between the tar roof and the tile).

What If I Refinance?

As strange as it may seem, refinancing your property without a sale has no immediate tax consequences. You don't report new mortgages to the IRS. You will, however, have less equity to rely upon later, when you do sell and must pay capital gains taxes.

Beware of Becoming a Dealer in Real Estate

In this chapter we've assumed that you will have capital gains tax to deal with when you sell your property. However, if you buy and sell many properties, particularly within a single year, the IRS may qualify you as a dealer in real estate. A dealer is one who buys to sell—an investor is one who buys for appreciation and income. What that means is that your profits are now all considered to be personal income, not capital gains, and the tax can be significantly higher. Check with your accountant.

If I've conveyed to you nothing else in this chapter, I hope that I have given the impression that buying and selling real estate goes hand in hand with tax considerations. If you're a wise investor, you'll consult with your tax professional each time you plan to make a new move.

Conclusion

Working for Yourself

One of the great dreams of most Americans is to own their own businesses—to be entrepreneurs, to work for themselves, and to have no boss over them. And to make a fortune doing it. Real estate is perhaps the last field that offers this opportunity to everyone.

Some move into this field by getting their real estate licenses and then becoming agents. As of this date, there are nearly a million agents in this country.

Far more, however, quietly invest in real estate and reap the benefits over time. Indeed, the millionaire next door probably became wealthy through real estate investments.

Although no one knows how many people invest in real estate, well over 65 million people (families) own property in this country. A good many of them own more than one property. A good many of those have a net worth in excess of a million dollars.

Can you be one of these?

Get Started Early

There's the old story of a farmer who planted a small orchard every time he and his wife had a child. They had six children and six orchards. As the family grew, so did the trees. And when the children reached their maturity, the farmer gave each of them an orchard that they could then maintain or sell or otherwise use as they saw fit.

Getting wealthy in real estate is doing something similar. It's best started when you're young, in your thirties or forties. (I'll have some good news for us more mature folks shortly.) Then you have the time to "plant" your investments. If you're 35 years old and you buy one property a year for 20 years, by the time you're 55 you'll have 20 properties, several producing positive cash flow (because their value will have gone up while their mortgage will have gone down).

If you don't retire at 55, but keep on investing into your sixties, you'll have more properties, probably some paid off. And if you don't have any other retirement, not even Social Security, your properties should be able to provide you with a handsome enough income to keep you financially well supported in your later years.

On the other hand, maybe you've been busy doing other things, and you're already 50, or 60, or even older. Is it too late for you to start in real estate?

Not at all. Using the techniques we've discussed, you too can buy property with little to no cash. But unlike those who are younger and can afford to make a few mistakes along the way, you need to be more careful.

My suggestion is that if you're more mature and are seeking to get started investing in real estate, you be scrupulously careful about what you buy. Only purchase in areas where prices are rapidly appreciating, where there's a strong tenant base, and where you can afford to get in without straining your finances (even if this means moving to a different area). Even if you buy with little or no cash, you don't want to get an alligator that keeps eating at you. And keep a close eye open for flippables—properties you can quickly acquire and sell at a profit.

Finally, do not spend any of the money that you have set aside for your retirement on a speculative investment (as a rental house may be). Remember, no investment is risk free. You should only take risks with money you can afford to lose.

Getting Money out of Your Real Estate

In Chapter 12 we discussed the tax advantages of harvesting your real estate investments by selling or trading. If you have multiple properties and you need cash, this may be an excellent method of obtaining it. However, there is another way. Refinancing.

In Chapter 3 we discussed methods of financing, and many of these also apply to refinancing. Here, however, I want to talk about the whole concept of refinancing to cash out your properties.

Again, think of the analogy of an orchard. For a real orchard, the crop might be plums or peaches or apples. For a financial orchard, the crop is cash.

After you've owned a property for a time, you can reasonably expect it appreciate in value. The appreciation will be greater or smaller, sooner or later, depending on a wide variety of factors such as inflation, the housing supply, demand from buyers/tenants, and so forth. (We discussed this in the early chapters.). However, whether the market is bad or good, over time you can expect your equity in your property rise.

As soon as your equity exceeds 20 percent of the value, to be conservative, you can think about harvesting some cash. (Remember, lenders like you to maintain at least 20 percent equity when you refinance, although this is not a hard and fast rule.) Let's say that your equity is 30 percent of the value. You should easily be able to obtain a second mortgage either from a private lender (many advertise regularly in the papers or over the Internet) or from an institutional lender for 10 percent. And if your equity has increased, chances are the rental income you can get from the property has also increased, which should pay for the new mortgage.

If the property is worth $100,000, your equity is 30 percent, and you get a new 10 percent loan, that's $10,000 you can put into your pocket. And remember, there's no tax to pay on a refinance. You only pay on your gain when you sell.

Then let the property sit and grow for another few years. Eventually, it's going to be worth $120,000. Now your equity is once again up, to about 33 percent. So you harvest again, refinance, and pull another $12,000 out.

You wait, the property equity grows, and when it's up to $150,000 in value, you harvest yet again, pulling $15,000 more out.

And so it goes. As your property gains in value, you can pull a portion of your equity out. If you have a big gain over a couple of years, you can pull money out each year. If it takes longer, you might have to wait several years to harvest your money.

Now multiply this times 10 properties. You should be able to see very quickly how, even in a short time, you can begin living off your real estate (in addition to any positive cash flow from rental income). And best of all, your real estate is a renewable resource. Like a tree, it keeps growing and growing with ever more crops ready to harvest.

Keeping a Business Perspective

It's always a good idea to think of yourself as a businessperson. Indeed, the government encourages you to think this way by the many deductions it will allow you on your real estate investments. (Note: The following tax deductions are for illustration only. You may or may not be able to claim them in your particular situation. Check with your accountant.)

For example, you can have an office from which you conduct your real estate business. And a separate phone line. Thus, when you advertise for rentals, the business phone gets the call in your office. And when tenants come to you to pay rent, you can meet them in your office.

This office does not necessarily need to be in a commercial building. It can be one room (perhaps an extra bedroom) in your own home. If you use it exclusively for business purposes, you may be entitled to deduct your costs (rent or depreciation, utilities, phone, and so on) from your taxes. (Note: When you sell, you may need to recapture any depreciation taken on a home office. Check with your accountant.)

Business cards can be a deduction as can mileage to and from your rentals. Even a car can be a deduction, if you use it primarily for business purposes.

And, depending on your personal income, you may even be able to deduct some losses on your real estate (see the previous chapter).

All of which is to say that when you become a real estate investor, you enter a far different world from a salaried wage earner. You become a true businessperson, with all the perks that affords.

Get Started Now!

So what's holding you back?

Is it lack of cash, income, or credit? We've seen how to get around these problems in this book.

Is it lack of time? Remember, even though as an investor you're your own boss, you don't need to put in a lot of time. Indeed, most real estate investing is best done as a part-time activity. Most people who have become wealthy in real estate worked at it only on weekends and the occasional evening.

Is it lack of enthusiasm? Even if you have no other opportunities, here's something that you can work on right now.

If you follow the techniques we've discussed, you'll find it's easy. Remember, you don't need to be a great salesperson, you don't need a formal education, you don't need to be cunning. All that you really need is persistence and the same good luck that favors most of us.

I believe real estate is America's greatest investment opportunity. And once you get your feet wet investing in it, I think you'll feel the same way.

APPENDIX 1

Solving Credit Problems

There are many institutional low-down and no-down mortgages out there. However, what all of these low- or nothing-down financing plans have in common (besides usually requiring you to live in the property) is the demand that you have good credit.

But, what if you don't have such good credit? What if you've been in a situation where you've had a few late payments? Or maybe you've defaulted on a loan? Or you've had a bankruptcy? Or, what's considered the most heinous of all credit problems, you've had a foreclosure?

In Appendix 1 we'll look at how credit problems can affect your ability to get real estate financing. Then we'll look at ways to get around these roadblocks. Note: We're going to assume you're intending to initially occupy the property yourself, as explained in Chapters 1 through 3.

Why Should a Lender Offer You a Loan?

If a lender grants you a mortgage, it is offering you hundreds of thousands of dollars toward the purchase of a home. This is probably the biggest financing deal that most Americans ever make. And what does that lender want in return? To know that you'll repay the debt, with interest.

If the lender can be perfectly assured you'll repay, as agreed, you'll quickly get the financing. If the lender has some doubts, then there may be some delays, and the lender could ask for a higher interest rate to offset a higher risk. But, if the lender believes that there's a serious chance you won't repay, you simply won't get your mortgage.

When you apply for a mortgage, you'll be asked to fill out a standard loan application. It has about 60 questions on it and identifies whole categories of your personal finances including the following:

- Your income and expenses
- Your reserves (money in the bank)
- Your current assets
- Your long-term debt
- And more

As part of that application you'll also give identifying information such as your full name, past addresses, and Social Security number. Based on this info, the lender will run a three-bureau credit check (also sometimes called a "standard factual").

There are three national credit bureaus:

- Experion
- Transunion
- Equifax

Among the three, they contain input from many other smaller credit-reporting agencies around the country. If you've paid your bills on time, that will show up on this report. And if you haven't paid bills on time and have other problems, they will show up as well.

Financial Profiling

It might seem to be a simple matter to take a look at a credit report and say, "This person has good credit—we'll give him a mortgage." Or, "That person has bad credit—we'll deny him a mortgage."

However, it's not that easy. While it's only common sense that whether you paid in the past is a likely indicator of whether you will pay in the future, exactly how does your earlier credit performance indicate future behavior? How does a lender know with any certainty what you'll do? Maybe you were out of work and had credit problems. But, now you've got a solid job and will perform as agreed. Maybe you were going through a divorce or an illness. Now you're more stable.

A credit report is only figures on a piece of paper. How does the lender evaluate it?

The answer is that lenders rely, in part, on special companies to do that evaluation for them. The biggest of these is FICO (Fair Isaac) in California. FICO analyzes your credit report and then gives you a score between 300 and 900. The higher your score, the better a borrower you're likely to be. The lower your rating, the more likely you'll be late on payments or default on your loan.

If you've applied for a mortgage recently, chances are you have a FICO score, and you can learn what it is. Simply go to *www.myfico.com* online. (You can also obtain it through *www.experion.com*.) For $12.95 (current price) you'll get your score. The FICO site also provides all sorts of information on how your FICO score is determined and gives a few clues on how to raise it.

We've been glossing over this, but presumably we're talking about the company that will actually offer you the mortgage, right? It's the company that looks at your FICO score and determines whether or not to extend financing.

Wrong! As it turns out in today's real estate mortgage market, the company whose name appears on the mortgage documents you get is ultimately nothing more than a servicer. It originates the loan and then collects payments from you. The actual money usually comes from one of two sources, Fannie Mae or Freddie Mac (called secondary lenders). These are huge quasigovernment corporations that loan billions on real estate. They are the ones that give thumbs up or thumbs down on your mortgage. Here's how it works.

A Quick Look at the Underwriting Process

You apply for a mortgage through a mortgage broker. She sends your application to a mortgage lending company. The mortgage company forwards your application to, for example, Fannie Mae's underwriting department. The underwriters look at your application and your FICO score and then apply a profile of their own. Depending on how it all comes out, Fannie Mae tells the mortgage company whether and what kind of a loan it will accept. The mortgage company passes the info onto your mortgage broker who lets you know. That's the overall process.

Profiling? Did someone say profiling?

We're talking financial profiling here (although most lenders never use that term). The underwriters have a database of hundreds of thousands of successful and unsuccessful borrowers. From that database they create profiles of what successful mortgage applicants will look like. Then they try to fit you into one of these profiles.

Thus the underwriters have your credit report, your credit score, and their own profiles based on past financial history to determine how you'll fare. Even so, they rarely give a simple pass or fail. Rather, you'll end up with a letter grade, typically from A to D.

Mortgage lenders see borrowers in a range between those that they are positive will repay, whom they call "prime," and those that they are worried will not repay, called "sub-prime." Prime borrowers have no credit problems, strong income, and lots of cash in the bank. They are also the "A" borrowers. Everyone else is sub-prime and is rated from "A−" down to "D."

Here's a brief description of a how the letter rating system typically works. Keep in mind this applies to no particular lender, but rather is a composite. Each lender has its own yardstick.

Rating Borrowers

Rating	Description
A	Most credit worthy.
A−	One unpaid bill, under $1000, turned in to collection or no more than one late payment of over 60 days or two late payments of over 30 days in credit cards or installment debt, all within the last two years. No bankruptcies or foreclosures on record (at least in the previous seven years).
B	Within the past year and a half has up to four late payments of no more than 30 days in credit cards or installment debt. May have had a bankruptcy or a foreclosure concluded at least two years before applying for loan.

C   Within the past year has had up to six late payments of no more than 30 days in credit cards or installment debt. May have accounts currently in collection, but mortgage may be granted if they are no more than $5000 and paid in full by the time the mortgage is funded. Mortgage funds may be used to clean up these debts. If there is a bankruptcy, it was resolved at least a year before applying for the mortgage. If there is a foreclosure, it was concluded at least two years before applying for the loan.

D   Many current late payments, several accounts in collection, and judgments against. These can be paid off from the proceeds of the new mortgage. If there was a bankruptcy, it was concluded more than six months before the application for the new mortgage. If there was a foreclosure, it was concluded at least two years before applying for loan.

You can be an excellent credit risk, yet by doing something as simple as carrying high balances on a couple of credit cards, you might lower your rating. On the other hand, you may be a terrible credit risk, but by presenting your credit information in just the right light, you may secure surprisingly good financing.

TRAP

Many people are surprised to learn that even a few late payments can seriously affect their ability to get real estate financing. The attitude, "I'll pay when I'm good and ready," may sound defiant against a creditor whom you dislike, but when those late payments show up on your credit report, your future mortgage lender wonders if you'll say the same thing to it.

Obviously, if you're a prime "A" borrower, the best loans are available to you. However, if you're in a lesser category then, in theory, other types of financing are available to you. A few years back it was simply a matter of increasing the interest rate. Prime borrowers got the market rate. Sub-prime borrowers had to contend with a higher rate. For example, if you were a "D" borrower, your LTV might be lower, and you might have to pay as much as 5 percent higher on your mortgage.

Severe defaults by sub-prime borrowers over the last few years, however, have derailed many of the programs that catered to them.

Today, if you're severely sub-prime you might have trouble finding a mortgage. Check with your mortgage broker to see what's available at the time you're looking.

Can I Improve My Credit Rating?

That's the question many people would love to have answered. Most scoring companies suggest that it's possible to improve your score in only a modest way. For example, FICO has pointed out that applying for credit too many times (more than three, for example) within months of applying for your mortgage could lower your score. Thus, the suggestion is not to apply for credit unless and until you actually need it.

TIP

Simply checking on your credit by buying a credit report directly from a credit bureau should not count as applying for credit. For this reason, most financial advisers suggest you check on your credit report once or twice a year, just to be sure there are no errors present.

I've been observing the mortgage industry and how credit scoring and credit categories are built, and the following are my own observations. There's no guarantee that doing any of the following will improve your standing. Yet, on the other hand, it just might.

Down Payment

Presumably you want to put as little as possible down. From the lender's perspective, however, the more you put down, the better. The reason is that the more you have invested into the property of your own money, the less likely you are to let it go to foreclosure if the market turns down or you lose your job. The more you have invested, presumably, the harder you'll fight to keep the home.

If you want to better your likelihood of getting financing, try to increase your cash down. Even a small increase may make a difference.

Cash Sources

Another consideration is where you get the money for the down payment. Ideally it will be your own money earned over the years and set aside as savings. Borrowing the down payment can be a problem. Borrowing the down suggests to the underwriter that you really can't afford the property. Let the lender know you're borrowing your down payment, and you might be scuttling the loan.

Therefore, if you need to borrow money that you intend to use as part of the down payment, do it well in advance of applying for the mortgage (at least six months). That way the money will be seen as part of a savings account, and the loan will be long established. In other words, you won't be borrowing specifically to make the home purchase.

Gifts for the down payment from relatives are acceptable. These must, however, be legitimate gifts. They can't be given with such strings attached as you'll repay the gifter so much a month and when you sell the property you'll repay the balance in full. In that case, they are nothing more than disguised loans.

In the past many underwriters insisted that those offering gifts as part of the down payment and closing costs cosign the mortgage and also qualify for it. This effectively nixed the deal in many cases. That requirement, however, has recently been removed for many federally underwritten mortgages. Today a gift with a simple gift letter may suffice. Check with your lender

Money Held Aside

If you have money left in the bank after you make the down payment and take care of the closing costs, lenders will like you. Ideally lenders would like to see at least three months or more worth of monthly expenses. If you have only a month or two, you could be turned down or, more likely, may be asked to accept a smaller mortgage.

Thus, you can usually improve your credit standing by holding a couple of months of cash in the bank. Not easily done, but something to consider.

Ouch! Bad Debts

The credit companies check the public records to see if you have had any bankruptcies or foreclosures. They also look for any loans you have that are now in collection.

The credit agencies also try to determine whether you are delinquent in any of your Trade Lines (credit cards). Any adverse notation can be cause for not issuing the mortgage.

Therefore, if you're behind in payments, catch up before applying for the mortgage. Try to stay caught up for at least a year before applying so your delinquencies will show up as old rather than recent. Old delinquencies are much easier to forgive.

However, be aware that frequent and severe delinquent payments can also sink you, even if you're caught up now. The best policy is to preserve your good credit by always paying on time. If you can't make the payments, don't borrow the money.

A recent bankruptcy can sink you. However, if it's been more than two years, it may simply be ignored by the lender. (Bankruptcies are carried on your credit report for a minimum of seven years and often much longer.) A foreclosure listed on your credit, however, is almost never ignored. Lenders don't like to offer mortgages to people who have in the past allowed their homes to sink into foreclosure.

Stating Your Income

Your income is obviously how much money you make before taxes. It includes such things as alimony. If both spouses have a long history of career work, their entire salaries may be counted. On the other hand, if one spouse works only part time or has only a short work history, only a portion of his or her income may be counted. Your expenses include PITI (principal, interest, taxes, and insurance) on the property plus living expenses plus other debt.

When filling out a mortgage application, it usually pays to emphasize length and continuity. For example, you're a teacher who has gotten his first job in years just a month ago. The lender is bound to wonder if you will succeed at the work. However, if you note that you were a teacher with five years experience a decade ago, before leaving the field to help raise children, it can help put your application in a whole new and better light.

Help for the Self-Employed

The method by which you receive your income is important, too. If you work for an employer and receive wages (meaning a W-2 form at the end of the year), you get preference mainly because it is easy to verify your income and because, presumably, you have something called "job security." (The only way a lender can determine this is by asking your employer what your chances for future employment are—a question frequently asked.)

On the other hand, if you're self-employed, you may be turned down without further consideration. Sometimes prime loans simply will not be granted to self-employed individuals. In other cases you will be asked to produce the last two years of your 1040 federal tax filings. The concern here is actually verifying your income—you could submit false records. (Today many lenders are capable of verifying income directly with the IRS.) And when you are self-employed, unless you can show a long work history, you are presumed to be at risk of job loss.

Thus, if you can show income as an employee, you're usually far better off than if you can show only income as a self-employed person.

The amount of your income will have to be big enough to allow you to make the mortgage payments and leave sufficient monies over for all your living expenses plus your taxes. Complex formulas for "front end" (the ratio of your house payment including principal, interest, taxes, and insurance to your income) as compared to "back end" (the ratio of your total monthly payments to your gross income) are used. These formulas are beyond the scope of this book and, besides, they aren't at all helpful to most borrowers when trying to figure out if they will qualify for a mortgage.

Suffice it to say, you need as much income as possible. Thus, if possible, it is usually a good idea to pay off any short-term debt (such as from

credit cards) before applying for a mortgage. That way you increase
your income (less is set aside to pay for the short-term debt), and you
may have a better chance of qualifying. On the other hand, the more
of your available cash you use to pay off debt, the less you will have available for a down payment and closing costs. Again, it's a tradeoff.

Too Many or Too Few Credit Cards?

What are the recent balances on all of your trade lines (credit
cards), the average balances over the past six months, and how close
are you to your credit limits?

The underwriters are concerned about people who live on their
credit. They don't mind if you borrow, so long as you have plenty
of credit left. On the other hand, if you have 10 credit cards and
have borrowed to the limit on all of them, it suggests a poor money
manager . . . and someone who might not be able to make mortgage payments.

Therefore, if you are borrowed out, before applying for a mortgage consider paying down or at least consolidating some of your
outstanding debt. Perhaps you can obtain a single loan that will not
only pay off all existing debt, but leave you a considerable buffer of
unused credit on your cards. It will certainly look better to your
mortgage underwriter. But do it well in advance (at least six months)
of your mortgage application. (Keeping your credit borrowing
under 50 percent of your maximum credit limit is a good idea.)

How Old Are Your Credit Lines?

Lenders want to know that you've been successfully borrowing for a
long time. That tells them that you're a good money manager. To determine this they look at your oldest trade lines. The older the better.

TRAP

Generally speaking, more than three to six credit
applications in six months is likely to be a mark against
you.

Similarly, if you open too many new credit cards or other charge accounts, it looks suspiciously like you may be planning to borrow a lot of money and leave the country. The underwriters check your most recent new accounts. An account opened in the previous three months is not good.

A good balance between credit cards, car loans, personal finance companies, and other installment loans is best. You don't want a lot of any of these or even a huge total. But the fact that you've got a car loan, three credit cards, and perhaps a department store card, and you've maintained reasonable balances all suggest you're a good credit manager. And that's what the underwriters actually want the most.

Chances are that if you have reasonably good credit, you won't be turned down for a new mortgage. Rather, if you're not approved outright, you'll be given a conditional approval provided that certain conditions are fulfilled.

These conditions may be something as simple as providing missing documentation, such as a W-2 form or an old paycheck stub. Or they might be something more severe. The underwriter may feel that in order for you to meet their standards, you must increase your down payment and, accordingly, reduce the amount you are borrowing.

That's a lot to ask. You may not have any more cash and may need the maximum loan. If that's the case, the answer could be, "Sorry."

What If Your Bad Credit Is the Result of Mistakes?

That depends on what the trouble is. It's a mistaken belief that you can have all bad credit "fixed." Companies that offer to fix or make any credit problem simply disappear, particularly if they charge you a hefty fee for doing it, may be nothing more than scams.

On the other hand, today there are many credit fixers out there who can, indeed, improve your credit in the sense of correcting mistakes. These are companies, however, that do for you (and for a fee) what you can do for yourself.

For example, if your credit is bad for the following reasons, it probably can be fixed.

Common Credit Mistakes

- Wrong name or address is on the report.
- Wrong Social Security number is on the report.
- Creditor has a paid-off loan still showing as owed.
- Property was redeemed, yet it shows up as a foreclosure.
- You did not file for bankruptcy, yet a bankruptcy shows up against you.

Mistakes and errors can be corrected. But it takes time and effort to do so. Credit fixers, for a fee, will go through all the hassle of correcting the mistakes and errors. Their fees are not small but, given the difficulties in correcting these sorts of problems, may be well worth it!

On the other hand, if you have credit that is truly bad, it cannot be fixed. This would include:

Bad Credit That Cannot Be Fixed

- Foreclosure
- Late or missed payments (without a reason)
- Bankruptcies

The best advice is simply to pay all your bills on time. Nothing messes up your credit quicker than late payments. Yet, these often result from carelessness or forgetfulness. Keep all bills in a special spot, and make it a point to pay them at least once a week. This is probably the simplest yet most effective step you can take toward preserving your good credit.

Pay First, Argue Later?

If you're concerned that a creditor may turn you in to a credit-reporting agency over a disputed bill, one way to avoid this problem is to pay the creditor in full. And then sue it in small claims court for the amount. You often stand an excellent chance in small claims court of recouping your money, and since this requires the creditor to spend time in court, plus perhaps give back the money, it teaches a creditor a real lesson.

Lenders are human, too, and they realize that sometimes credit-worthy people get into trouble. If your explanation shows that you at least tried to solve the problem and, perhaps even more important, that the problem was isolated and isn't likely to happen again, you may very well be able to get the financing you want, even a prime mortgage!

The best way to do this is to be up front with the lender. Don't wait for the problem to surface as part of your credit report. Get it out front. And provide the lender with a clearly written letter of explanation. If you have late payments, explain why they were late. If you defaulted on a loan, give all the details and include verifying information. If you had a foreclosure, explain how it occurred and why circumstances are different now.

Credit Bureaus Do Make Mistakes

As many as a third of all credit reports contain an error of some kind. Even if the error is the fault of the credit bureau, it can still cause you to be declined for a mortgage. When that happens, you need to get out and correct that error. (This is another good reason to order your own credit report early on. You can discover if there are errors and take steps to correct them.)

Generally speaking, the best approach to take in correcting errors is to obtain proof that it is indeed an error then write to the credit-reporting agency offering the proof and demanding the error be corrected. The credit agency must investigate your request and take action within a month or two.

The trick is getting the proof. What's usually accepted is a letter or document from the lender that reports the bad credit saying it was a mistake. Or, in the case of mistaken identity, it's a matter of presenting irrefutable evidence that you're who you are and not the other person the credit company thinks you are. Birth certificates, driver's license, escrow company ID statements, and so forth can help here.

Remember, the basic method of correcting bad credit is twofold. First, you have to write a letter explaining the problem and why it's the creditor's fault or an error in reporting by the credit bureau. Second, you have to submit documentation proving what you say.

How soon the credit bureau will correct the mistake depends on your proof. If the original creditor who reported the problem now reports an error, the agency will normally remove the offending report within 30 days.

On the other hand, if your proof tends to be your word against the lender's, who refuses to admit an error, it's a different story. The credit report agency is generally required to insert your letters of explanation along with the bad report and may make your substantiating documentation available to those who ask for reports.

The credit agency, however, doesn't usually take sides. In a disputed case they probably will not remove the offending incident. It will stay on your report usually for up to seven years.

For more information on how to correct an error in your credit report, write to the Federal Trade Commission at CRC-240, Washington, D.C., 20580 or phone them at 1-877-FTC-HELP (382-4357).

How Do I Get a Copy of My Credit Report?

It's a good idea to get a copy of your own credit report in advance of applying for a mortgage. That way you get to see what the lender will see and prepare for it. You are allowed to obtain at least one copy of your credit report each year. You probably will want to get it from one of the big credit reporting agencies. The cost is minimal.

Transunion	800-888-4213	*www.tuc.com*
Experian (formerly TRW)	888-397-3742	*www.experian.com*
Equifax	800-685-1111	*www.equifax.com*

It's Not My Fault

Sometimes it's the truth. Perhaps you cosigned for someone else on a car. They ran off with the car and never made the payments. You were stuck with either making payments for five years on a car you didn't have and couldn't sell or simply refusing. You refused.

This shows you had the good sense not to get in debt over your head. However, it also shows that you had the bad sense to cosign for someone else. Further, given tough circumstances, instead of plodding on and making payments, you'll bail out—something that makes good sense to you, but which lenders don't particularly like to see.

You got in over you head. You live in California, but bought property in Oklahoma just before the oil price bust of the mid-1980s. You couldn't sell or rent it and weren't there to take care of it. Consequently, you lost it to foreclosure.

But that was years ago, and it was rental real estate. Here and now you're trying to buy a home in which you plan to live. The circumstances are different. Maybe the lender will agree.

I Was Ill

This may be acceptable if you have a long history of excellent credit broken by a short period, say six months, of poor credit, followed by another long period (at least two years) of good credit. This explanation is particularly helpful in explaining late payments.

I Had a Divorce or Death in the Family

Here again, you normally must show that this happened some time ago, and since that time, you've had excellent credit. This is particularly useful when you defaulted on loans. You had a big setback in your life, but now you're back in the saddle, as evidenced by at least two year's worth of good credit history.

A Natural Disaster

There was a tornado that destroyed not only your home, but also the factory where you work. You had no place to live and no way to earn income. Naturally you had to let your house go into foreclosure. But since then the factory's been rebuilt, and you're back at work. You're ready to start again by buying a house.

When You're Just Getting Started

You want to buy a home, but you're young and new to the game and haven't established much credit. That's a problem. In order to give you a mortgage, a lender has to establish your money management patterns. It does that by seeing how successfully you've paid back money that you've previously borrowed. But, if you've never borrowed, the lender can't establish a pattern. And in the world of borrower profiles, that can leave you out in the cold.

That doesn't mean, however, that you can't otherwise establish your credit and get a mortgage. Indeed, having no credit is just an inconvenience. If you make the proper efforts, you can establish a good credit record and be years ahead of the individual who starts off with lots of bad reports.

Establishing credit is not hard. But begin at least six months, hopefully a year or more, before you plan on applying for a mortgage. It will take time to establish a good credit history. It can't be done overnight.

Establishing Credit

The first thing you should do is to go to the bank where you do business (not having credit doesn't mean you don't have a checking and savings account) and apply for a debit card. As you probably know, this is like a credit card, only based on your assets in the bank. Today many banks offer these virtually automatically to their customers.

Once you have the debit card, use it frequently to establish that you can manage such an item. Also, be scrupulous to see that you never bounce your own checks and can always cover any checks from others that you deposit. Ask your bank to establish a small line of credit to cover your checking account, just in case you should be short. This overdraft credit line is also often just an automatic for good, long-standing customers.

Once you have an overdraft account and a debit account, ask your bank for a credit card. Almost all banks offer them. With your good standing in the bank, it should again be automatic.

Once you get that credit card, you're halfway home. Go out and charge halfway to the limit. Then pay it back promptly. Pay off all your charges each month for three months, and you've established a credit history.

Very shortly other credit card offers should start appearing in the mail. Apply for two others (no more, no less). Charge a few things on these, and make regular monthly payments.

Now, go back to your bank and ask for a noncollateral loan—a line of credit. Say you want to buy furniture or a used car. You have your history at the bank, plus your new credit cards, plus the fact that you have no bad credit. Again, it's a slam dunk.

Borrow a thousand dollars or so this way, put it in the bank, make regular payments on it and, after a few months, pay it back.

Voilà. With the exception of longevity, you have just established the rudiments of prime credit. Age means how long you've had your trade lines. That first credit card you got? Keep it. It will age and, once it's two years old, you've started to satisfy the age portion.

TIP

You don't want just to establish credit. You want to establish good credit. Make all of your payments on time. If you're late or miss a payment, you'll establish credit all right, but it will be bad!

This plan is great if you've got the time to spend. But what if you want to get a mortgage right now? You don't have time to set up credit cards and installment loans. You want to buy a home, and you have to go with what you've got. But you have an empty credit history.

Establishing a Credit History

Actually, almost no one's credit history is truly empty. At worst it's usually just a case of not having thought of what to fill it with. Here are some suggestions for creating an instant credit history:

Friendly Loans—People who pay by cash often get loans from friends and family. If you paid these back on time, get your cancelled checks or other receipts. Have the person sign a statement showing the amount borrowed, the term, when regular payments were made, and when it was paid back. If the person from whom you borrowed it is able to put a corporate or business name on the statement, even better.

You might need to dig into your memory for some other account that similarly can be used to help establish your credit. Dig as deeply as possible. While none of these individually is as good as a long history of credit cards with prompt repayment, they can go a long way.

Receipts for Rent and Utilities—You must have lived somewhere and, if you didn't own, you rented. If you paid rent by check, get those cancelled checks. They should show a steady pattern of regular payments. Better still, get a letter from your current and previous landlords stating that you made your rent payments on time. Also have the landlord state the amount to establish that you can handle a large monthly payment.

You also had to have electricity, water, garbage, gas, phone, and probably cable TV. You paid for these. Again, look for cancelled checks. Also, call up the companies and ask them for letters of recommendation. Many utility companies will do this almost automatically if you've had a good payment history for one year.

Get a Cosigner

If you don't have the credit history, find someone who does, and make them a partner. Relatives are usually opportune choices. Good friends, even business associates, are also likely candidates. Remember, you don't need the cosigners to help you with the down payment or the monthly payments. You just need their good, established credit.

Keep in mind, however, that when someone cosigns with you, his or her credit is on the line. If you default (or worse, if you lose the property to foreclosure), it will reflect badly on his or her credit. It will be as if the cosigner was late on payments or lost the property. For this reason, keep in mind that most savvy people will refuse to cosign for anyone, even close relatives.

To induce other people to cosign for you, you may want to give them an ownership position in the property. You may want them to have their names appear both on the deed and on the mortgage. That way, should you for some reason stop making payments or go into foreclosure, they can step in and take over—and possibly save the property. This can be a strong inducement to a reluctant cosignor.

Most lenders will want the cosigners on the mortgage in any event. So, it's just one more simple step to include them on the deed. Once the cosignors are on the deed, however, they can tie up the property and potentially keep you from selling. To protect your interests, you will want to have an attorney draw up an agreement specifying exactly what interests they have (none, except in the event you default), what say they have in managing or selling the property (again, presumably none, unless you have problem), and what percentage of the profit they will receive in the event the property is sold (again, presumably none). This will help protect your interests.

APPENDIX 2

Selling Short

In any market an investor can get "upside down." That simply means that you owe more on your property than it's worth. If you try to sell at the market price, not only will you not receive any money out of the sale, you might have to put in money out of your own pocket just to make the sale!

Being upside-down happens to investors more in down markets, where prices drop and there are too many rentals and not enough tenants (and where those would-be tenants are out of work and can't pay their rent). However, even in strong markets, investors can get too much financing on the property so that they have little, none, or even negative equity. When they throw in the costs of selling (commission, title insurance, escrow fees, and so on), many investors discover they're upside-down.

If you're upside down and you find you must sell right away, take heart. You should get some immediately useful answers in this appendix. (Of course, you should also reread Chapter 6 on tips for avoiding getting in this situation!)

There are a number of things you can do immediately when the rental and housing markets are against you and you're upside down.

Contact Your Lender

Talking is good advice. If you're behind in your payments, or if you need your lender to make a concession on your loan (accept a short payoff, or less than owed), talking to your lender transforms you from an impersonal name on a sheet of paper into a person. You've got a personality; you've got warmth, humor, and value. In short, it's a lot harder to beat up on someone you know than on a complete stranger, even for a lender.

As soon as you realize you're upside-down and need to sell, contact your lender. Find out its policy. Find out if it can help you restructure your loan (many lenders will work hard to do this).

Contacting your lender, however, can be more difficult than it at first seems. After all, most lenders are giant institutions. How do you find the one person among hundreds of employees, perhaps thousands, who will respond to your needs?

Turn it around. If you don't contact your lender, and you stop making your mortgage payments, your lender will contact you.

And the person making that contact may not be nearly as pleasant as the person you'll find if you go looking yourself.

If your lender is a local institution, such as a bank, often the best place to start is a local branch office. If you know the employees there, they often can direct you to the right person.

If your lender doesn't have a local office, then start calling and work your way through the system. You may have to go through several at least partial explanations to get through to someone who will listen, understand, and, if not commiserate, at least take notes for future reference.

In essence, what you tell your lender is that your property is not worth the mortgage amount, that you're having trouble making payments, and/or that you must sell.

Keep in mind that if you're up to date on your payments, most lenders don't want to talk to you. You're not a problem yet. Until you're at least several months behind in payments, many lenders won't deal with you seriously.

If you're several months behind, most lenders with whom you talk today will try to help you in several ways. They may be willing to allow you to miss payments for a period of time, if it appears you will be able to start making them again later on. (You're temporarily sick, for example.) Or they may restructure your loan, giving you lower payments. Or they might forgo interest for a period of time. After the real estate recession of the early 1990s, most lenders became quite adept at helping out troubled borrowers, even investors.

However, not all lenders are willing or able to help. You may just end up with a hardball lender that simply puts you into foreclosure. If that's the case, then you need to play hardball in return.

Offer a Short Sale

A *short sale* is a different tack. You suggest to the lender that the best way for both of you to get out of this predicament is for you to maintain the property, perhaps leaving it empty, but keeping it in good shape and finding a buyer. But the property is worth less than the mortgage and costs of sale. Therefore, in order for you to make the sales effort, the lender will have to agree to take less—a *short sale*.

Will lenders agree?

Probably not, at least not formally. What many savvy lenders will tell you is, "Keep on trying to sell, but if you find someone who is willing to buy in a short sale, we'll talk." That's about the extent of a commitment to a short sale you're likely to get from a lender. But it's a good start. Armed with nothing more than this, I would begin trying to sell the property at market value, which may be less than you owe.

If you are successful and do find a buyer ready, willing, and able to purchase on a short sale, write up the deal (or have your agent write it), get a deposit, and present it to the lender. From the lender's perspective, it's really tough to turn such a deal down, provided the amount short is not too great. After all, you're offering a way out that's neat and clean. If the lender refuses, there's the dirty way involving foreclosure and the costs of fixing up a property that the lender could get in damaged condition.

Don't try to get the lender to commit formally to a short sale and for a specific amount of money until you actually get a buyer in hand. Then you've got something to bargain with.

Hang on for Dear Life

Some investors, realizing that they can't sell or easily get out from under, have stubbornly hung on, renting at a loss and making up the difference in expenses each month out of their own pockets, sometimes a substantial amount. Others have borrowed money (from the bank or relatives)—all so that they could keep their losing property. They don't sell, and they do continue to make their payments. This might mean using up some of the retirement money or the kids' college funds. It could mean a lesser lifestyle for a while. But it could also mean avoiding foreclosure and the trauma of a forced property move. Sometimes investors just don't want to lose their "equity." They figure if they stay long enough, they'll get out what they have put into the property.

The trouble, however, is that it's usually possible to buy elsewhere in a better market and double or triple your equity in the time it takes to recoup it from an upside-down property. Quite frankly, I don't recommend staying on, unless there's a compelling reason to preserve your ownership of the property. Personally, I prefer moving on with my life, even if it means using one of the more dramatic solutions. I wouldn't like the trapped feeling of knowing that each month I was feeding an "alligator." Better to take a hit now and get on with things.

Some investors who are upside down with their properties choose to "walk." It's so much easier just to let the bank take the property back. Yes it is—until you want to buy another property. Then you may find that you've thrown the baby out with the bath water. The truth is that the worst possible thing you could do, in terms of personal finance, is to allow a foreclosure to occur. The reason is that the foreclosure could preclude you from getting financing on another property for a long time into the future.

The reason is that many mortgage lenders don't really care that much if you have a bankruptcy or if you don't make payments on your credit cards. They'll look aside if you don't pay your telephone bill or your water and electric bills. Just have a few good years of steady payments, and they'll forgive all the bad times.

But if they ever find out you let a property go to foreclosure, particularly a rental, most will look askance at giving you another mortgage. The reasoning here is that foreclosure is not like anything else. Lenders see it as a commitment on their part and yours. They will lend you more money than you could ever qualify for otherwise on your income. And they anticipate you will pay it back honorably, no matter what.

All of which is to say that if you ever hope to buy another property in the future, protect your mortgage credit. Find a way to pay off the mortgage. Get yourself off the hook. Don't ever consider walking. If you do, you'll find it very difficult to get another mortgage in the future. Of course, this is not to say that you can't ever get any kind of mortgage. Some lender may get desperate and give you a loan.

And there are always the "equity lenders" who will lend a smaller (around 65 percent) percentage of a property's value. They don't care who's applying for the loan. Some don't even conduct a credit check. (Some hope you actually won't make payments so they can foreclose!) But equity lenders require that you make a huge down payment, and they charge much higher interest. They are a poor alternative.

By the way, don't think you can sneak by a lender. Every mortgage loan application asks if you have *ever* had a foreclosure. Most, today, also ask if you have ever given a deed in lieu of foreclosure (considered bad, but not nearly so bad as foreclosure). If you fudge on the application, the foreclosure could show up on a credit report. (Mortgage lenders use the most sophisticated nationwide credit reporting available.) Even if it doesn't show up and you do get the loan, should you later default and it turns out that you lied on your application, you could be liable for serious civil and/or criminal penalties.

Purchase Money Mortgages

Usually it's only the property that's collateral for the mortgage. However, unless you obtained the mortgage as part of the purchase price, and only in those states that have "purchase money mortgage" laws, even if you walk, the lender could go to court and obtain a deficiency judgment against you personally for any money it loses by taking the property back. This judgment would follow you.

In most cases it is possible to avoid foreclosure. It may not be easy. You may need to change your plans or take actions you'd rather avoid. You may even have to sell an item you love, like a boat or car, to raise money for mortgage payments. You may have to do things you disdain, like borrowing from relatives. But where there's a will there's a way. And this is one case where finding the way will usually bring you a much happier financial future.

The last possible solution is to deed the property directly to the lender. The lender can then attempt to resell it. Yes, you won't get anything out of this deal, but it helps protect your credit and gives you an honorable way out. Besides, by now you have no equity anyhow.

Deed in Lieu

Why would a lender accept this option? Most don't, unless you make it more attractive to them. One person I know, after not making payments for three months and being threatened with foreclosure, called his lender and explained it this way: "If you accept a deed to the property in lieu of foreclosing, I'll have the nonpaying tenants out next week and you'll get the property back in good shape, ready to resell. If, however, you refuse, then I'll let them sit in the property, without making payments, for the five months it takes to foreclose in this state. During that time anything can happen—the hardwood floors might get ruined; holes might get put in the walls; windows, sinks, and toilets could get broken. Neighborhood gangs might even come in and tear up and graffiti the place. You'll get it back after foreclosure okay, but you may not like it!" The lender agreed immediately to accept a deed in lieu of foreclosure.

The investor played hardball.

Lenders are aware of this ploy and may go to court to get a restraining order against your damaging the property and to take the rents away from you. The order, however, can be hard to enforce, particularly if you abandon the property and damage occurs from vandalism after you leave and before the lender gets possession.

A *deed in lieu* should only be considered as a last resort.

APPENDIX 3

Little to No Cash Down Federal Loan Programs

The two biggest lenders in the country are Freddie Mac and Fannie Mae. These are quasipublic/private corporations that maintain a secondary market in home loans. When you get a loan through a mortgage broker or a bank (or a mortgage banker, which is a bank which only handles mortgages), chances are that loan is then sold to either Freddie Mac or Fannie Mae. The lender gets a fee for collecting your payments and now has money to lend on more mortgages.

In order to be able to transfer your loan to one of these lenders, it must be "conforming." That means it must conform to the underwriting standards of Fannie Mae or Freddie Mac. (Remember, in Chapter 9 we talked about underwriting.) Here the lender you're dealing with gets you to fill out an application. Then the application and a credit report are submitted to either Freddie Mac or Fannie Mae. They take a look at these along with your credit score, usually from FICO, and apply their own financial profiles. If you intend to occupy the property, they will usually issue a provisional approval or a rejection. If approved, you then can obtain one of the many different mortgage products they offer through lenders. If you don't intend to occupy property, but instead are buying it as an investor, you may be rejected out of hand, or a significantly larger (10 percent or more) down payment may be required.

Fannie Mae and Freddie Mae do not usually make loans directly to you, the borrower. Rather, you go through a direct lender or a mortgage broker.

It's hard to know just how much of the total home mortgage business in the country goes through these lenders. However, I have heard estimates with a high of as much as 90 percent. In any event it's a very large number. This is the reason that it's important to take a close look at the various affordable loans these two giants offer. (Remember, when we say "offer" we mean offer through conventional lenders, not directly.)

Fannie Mae and Freddie Mac set the maximum loan amount you can get (currently $333,700, however this is frequently changed upward). They also determine the FICO score that will allow you to get prime loans (believed generally to be above 640.) They also have low-down and no-down programs as well as special programs for those who are credit-challenged.

The following information comes from Freddie Mac and Fannie Mae. It refers to various loan programs. Note that while all of these are similar, they have many important differences.

Freddie Mac and Fannie Mae change their mortgage plans frequently, hence this should not be considered written in stone. Also, although they both have plans for properties with one to four, or more, units the material here is just for single-family homes that you intend to occupy. Check with your mortgage broker or direct lender for more information.

For more information on the mortgages listed below, as well as background on Fannie Mae and Freddie Mac, check into *www.fanniemae.com* and *www.freddiemac.com.*

Ninety-Five Percent Mortgages—Freddie Mac

This is a mortgage plan, *Affordable Gold® 5,* designed for moderate- to low-income borrowers. It only requires a 5 percent down payment (95 percent LTV), and that is quite flexible (see below). It is available on a mortgage with terms of 15, 20, and 30 years. The maximum LTV (loan to value) is 95 percent.

Down Payment

The down payment requirement is 5 percent plus closing costs. However, under this financing "any acceptable source of nonaffordable mortgage products" may be used. This typically can include cash from relatives, gifts, and other sources.

In addition, "affordable seconds" (those approved by Freddie Mac) are also acceptable. In this case the TLTV (total loan to value) can be as high as 105 percent. In other words, if you don't have the cash to come up with the down payment and the closing costs, you can arrange a second mortgage to cover all of it.

Closing Costs

These include:

Prepaids

Escrows

Financing charges

Reserves

Most mortgage plans require that you maintain a reserve in cash in the event you run into difficulty making your payments. In this case the program "recommends" a reserve of one month, but does *not* require it.

Credit Qualifying

Freddie Mac does not disclose the minimum FICO score or its own scoring policy. However, it does indicate that your monthly debt-to-income ratio should not exceed 40 percent. This simply means that you should not be paying out more than 40 percent of your income in bills each month.

Interestingly, there is no maximum housing expense-to-income ratio required. In other words, under this plan it doesn't really matter how much of your income you will need to expend on the house. Rather, each case is judged on its own merits.

In order to qualify for this mortgage, you must enroll in a class on home buying education, which includes course work on money management. This is not really a bad thing for anyone.

Your income, however, may be limited to the median income in your area. In other words, this plan is not for high-income borrowers. It is intended to benefit those with relatively modest incomes. Exceptions to the income barrier are available in selected high-cost areas including those that follow.

- 120 percent of median in Bergen/Passaic, NJ; Portland, OR; and Seattle MSA (Metropolitan Statistical Area)
- 125 percent in Newark, NJ
- 135 percent in Boston MSA
- 140 percent in California
- 165 percent in New York MSA
- 170 percent in Hawaii
- No income limits are applicable in concentrated areas. Concentrated areas are those areas that HUD (U.S. Department of Housing and Urban Development) has indicated are either central cities or census tracts in which minorities predominate.

To find more information on targeted census tracts, check into *www.freddiemac.com/sell/affgold/index.html.*

Ninety-Seven Percent Mortgages—Freddie Mac

This mortgage ups the ante by allowing you to come in with as little as a 3 percent down payment (97 percent LTV). In addition you can get the money for closing costs from a variety of sources.

It is designed for low- to moderate-income families and, as a result, is limited to those whose incomes do not exceed the median for their areas. Exceptions are the same as for the 95 percent mortgage noted above.

Credit

- There is no maximum housing expense-to-income ratio.
- Your ratio of debt-to-income cannot be more than 40 percent.

- You must take a homebuyer education program.

- You are limited in the income you can have—see above.

Loan

A 97 percent LTV is available on 15-, 20-, and 30-year fixed-rate mortgages. (The minimum LTV is 95.01 percent.)

Affordable seconds are allowed to help you get the money for closing costs. However, the 3 percent down must be met by your own funds.

Alternate 97 Percent Mortgages—Freddie Mac

The *ALT 97® Mortgage* is similar to the plan noted above, except that there are no income or geographic limits.

It is designed for borrowers who have a strong credit profile but just don't have a lot of cash to be used for the down payment and closing costs. However, you may have access to nontraditional funds such as grants, loans from relatives or even employers, or outright gifts.

This mortgage is available for 15-, 20-, and 30-year fixed-rate mortgages.

The *Affordable Gold Alt 97SM* allows for a 97 percent mortgage. However, here the down payment does not have to come from your funds. It can come from an affordable second or other sources. The alternate funds can also be used to cover the closing costs.

You do, however, have to have exemplary credit. This includes:

- A high FICO score

- At least one month of reserves

You also must meet income and geographic requirements. See the 95 percent Affordable Gold mortgage above.

This mortgage is available for 15-, 20-, and 30-year fixed-rate mortgages.

For Credit-Challenged Borrowers—Freddie Mac

The *Affordable Merit Rate® Mortgage* is a mortgage for borrowers who have had some small credit problems and, because of it, are not considered "A" borrowers, but are instead considered "A−." (See Chapter 9 for definitions of "A" and "A−."

A− borrowers can quality for a mortgage, but at a higher interest rate. This loan is designed to help those borrowers get more affordable financing.

What makes this loan most interesting is that it not only offers a lower initial interest rate for some credit challenged borrowers, but, if the borrower is able to make 24 consecutive on-time payments to the mortgage within a four-year qualifying period, the interest rate is reduced by 1 percent. (Quite an incentive!)

Freddie Mac says of this loan that not only does it offer reduced loan rates, it also helps a borrower who might be having troubles to establish a record of good credit management.

Borrower Credit

- The borrower may be A−, which means that he or she was delinquent in a loan payment as many as two times over the previous 2 years.

- No more than two 30-day-or-more delinquencies in the prior 12 months.

- The borrower may have limited funds available for a down payment, hence relatively high LTV ratios.

- The borrower may have incurred lots of debt, provided there is a logical explanation such divorce, medical payments, or job loss.

- The borrower must be able to pay up on any late or unpaid debt, bringing it current.

- The monthly ratio of the borrower's debt payment to income cannot be greater than 50 percent.

- No bankruptcies within the past 24 months, and there can have been no foreclosure within the previous 36 months.

Loan Type

Freddie Mac offers this type of underwriting on a standard fixed-rate loan (15-, 20-, and 30-year) as well as mortgages with a balloon payment after 7 years (converting to an ARM—Adjustable Rate Mortgage). The loan is also available as an ARM. Affordable second financing may also be available in some cases.

The LTV may be as high as 90 percent for 30-year loans. However, in that case, 30 percent mortgage insurance is required. For 15- or 20-years loans, the LTV is a max of 90 percent with 25 percent mortgage insurance.

TRAP

Any mortgage with an LTV of over 80 percent requires private mortgage insurance. This insures the lender, not you the borrower, against loss. It insures the lender for the "top" of the mortgage, the first monies lost, anywhere from the top 5 to 40 percent. The greater the percentage, the higher the premium. You, the borrower, get stuck with the premium, which can be as much as half a percent or more of the mortgage annually. Mortgage insurance is a necessary evil. It costs us more money. But it allows us to get higher LTVs.

One Hundred Percent Mortgage—Freddie Mac

This is a special plan for borrowers who don't have the cash for a down payment or who have the cash but don't want to use it. It offers them a 100 percent LTV. It's a true "nothing down" plan.

In addition, under this mortgage plan, funds for purchasing the home may come from a gift from a related person.

Credit Requirements

- You must have excellent credit, meaning that you should be an "A" borrower (see definitions in Appendix 1).

- You can have had no bankruptcy or foreclosures, or have given a deed in lieu of foreclosure during the seven years prior to applying for this loan.

- Your maximum debt-to-income ratio can be 41 percent.

- No income limits (you don't have to be below a certain income level), except in the case of affordable second mortgages.

TRAP

When faced with foreclosure, some savvy borrowers will instead get the lenders to accept a deed back to them in lieu of going through with the foreclosure. This saves the lender time and money. It saves the borrower from having a foreclosure on his or her records. However, this became so rampant during the 1990s, that today having a "deed in lieu" on your record is tantamount to having a foreclosure. Today some lenders simply won't accept the deed in lieu, but will instead proceed through foreclosure.

The Loan

This is one of those mortgages that we tend to fantasize about. For those with limited funds and good credit, it's a dream. It allows:

- A 100 percent LTV (up to 103 percent with affordable seconds (for those who have limited incomes). The mortgage insurance must be 40 percent.

- Only 3 percent borrower funds, to be used for either the down payment or closing costs. The 3 percent can even be in the form of sweat equity!

TIP

"Sweat equity" simply means that you contribute your time and labor toward fixing up the property. That counts in lieu of cash toward the down payment, closing costs, or both.

- The seller of the property can contribute up to 3 percent of the borrower's closing costs and prepaid expenses.

- A related person can contribute up to 3 percent. (When gifts are made, there is usually a 5 percent down payment required from other sources. This is waived for this loan.)

The Property

As with all mortgages, the property must appraise for the sales price in order to get the high mortgage values. However, here the appraisal must in addition indicate that the property is not located in an area where real estate market values are declining.

Affordable Seconds— Freddie Mac

Freddie Mac now approves second mortgages. These can then be used to supplement your down payment or closing costs. They allow you to help qualify for a fixed-rate mortgage otherwise available through Freddie Mac.

This increases your flexibility when you're cash poor and are having trouble coming up with the down payment, but are otherwise a good credit risk. These are generally available to low- and moderate-income borrowers.

Note: While Freddie Mac purchases first mortgages, it does not purchase the second mortgage. That has to be arranged between yourself and your lender.

Fixed-Rate Mortgage— Fannie Mae

Just as Freddie Mac has done, Fannie Mae also has a large group of mortgages available for those who have affordability issues. Below is a summary of some of its more popular fixed-rate products.

Pledged-Asset mortgages offer up to 100 percent LTV financing. They are available to borrowers who show a large enough income to handle the mortgage, have good credit, but are short on cash. Fannie Mae's flagship here is its *Flexible 100®* mortgage plan.

Fannie 97® offers a 97 percent LTV mortgage. The 3 percent cash down, however, must come from the borrower's funds. However, the reserve requirement is only for one month's worth of mortgage payments.

There are, however, income and geographic area restrictions. And the borrower must participate in face-to-face education programs.

The loan can be from 15 to 30 years. Up to 38 percent of the borrower's monthly income can be used for housing costs and other debts, such as credit cards or student loans. Fully a third of the borrower's income can be aimed entirely at housing costs. Another similar mortgage, *Flexible 97®*, offers lower cost mortgage insurance.

Timely Payment Rewards® is a mortgage designed to help borrowers who have less than "A" creditworthiness. If the borrower goes two years without a 30-day delinquency within the first four years of the loan, he or she will receive an interest rate reduction. (It's handled automatically, so you don't have to write in for your reward!)

Interest First® is an unusual mortgage plan designed to help affordability by giving you the lowest possible mortgage payment. The way it works is unique.

Under *Interest First*, your mortgage payment is based entirely on interest for the first 15 years of the mortgage. Starting at year 16, your payment includes principal with the mortgage amortizing (fully paying off) within the remaining 15 years. Thus, the first half of the loan you pay interest only. The second half you pay interest and principal.

While this may seem like a terrific solution, it's important to note than in the initial years of a mortgage, the amount that goes to principal is not high. For example, in a $100,000 mortgage at 7 percent interest, the portion of the monthly payment that goes to principal in the first month is only $72. Thus, if the principal portion is eliminated, the monthly payment is reduced by only a few dollars.

On the other hand, if at year 16 you begin to make payments on both principal and interest, the mortgage payment could suddenly jump by as much as 20 percent, because you've only got 15 years to pay back the principal.

TIP

A savvy borrower would only keep this loan until year 15, then refinance or sell the property. The downside is that you're not contributing anything to equity return—you're not paying off the mortgage. At the end of year 15 you would owe as much as you did when you first obtained the financing.

Adjustable Rate Mortgages—
Fannie Mae

Fannie Mae also offers a large array of adjustable rate mortgages (ARMs). These offer 3-, 5-, 7-, and 10-year fixed interest rate periods. After the initial fixed-rate period, the mortgage converts to an adjustable.

LIBOR indexed mortgages often offer a six-month teaser. The LIBOR index is advertised as promoting against wide swings in interest rates that could adversely affect the borrower. (Indeed, the LIBOR has historically been a stable barometer of the interest rate market.)

Two-Step® is a mortgage with only one adjustment. Fannie Mae's *ARM 975* adjusts after seven years. Its *ARM 1029* adjusts after five years. In both cases the new interest rate is determined based on the weekly average of 10-year Treasury securities (adjusted to a constant maturity), plus a margin.

TIP

The 10-year Treasury securities index is widely used for adjusting fixed-rate mortgages, ever since the demise of the 30-year security.

Fannie Mae also offers another unusual and potentially beneficial product: its 7-year balloon mortgage.

Here, the monthly payments are based on a 30-year mortgage. However, the interest rate is based on a lower-rate 7-year mortgage. At year seven of the mortgage, the mortgage converts to a 23-year fixed-rate mortgage, based on market interest rates. Of course, the conversion assumes the borrower has maintained the mortgage in good standing during the first 7 years.

This is just a summary of some of the various loan programs of Fannie Mae and Freddie Mac. Take them to your mortgage broker and ask him or her about them. It's a good starting place!

APPENDIX 4

Mortgage Priority in Foreclosure

It's important to know the priority of mortgages involved in foreclosure, particularly when bidding at a foreclosure auction (see Chapter 12). Here, briefly, are the rules:

1. The mortgage recorded first has first priority (is superior).
2. Mortgages recorded later have lower priority (are junior).
3. Any mortgage can foreclose (first, second, third, etc.), but such foreclosure will not affect superior mortgages.

The best way to be sure that we're clear on this is to take an example. Tracy's house has three mortgages on it:

Third mortgage	$10,000
Second mortgage	$20,000
First mortgage	$70,000

Case 1. The first mortgage forecloses. Tracy's house brings $100,000 at the sale.

In this case the loan with the highest priority (the first for $70,000) gets paid off with the first money. Then the loan with the next priority (the second for $20,000) gets paid off. Finally, the loan with the least priority (the third for $10,000) gets paid off. There's no money left, so the owner-borrower gets nothing.

Case 2. As before, the first mortgage forecloses. Tracy's house brings $75,000 at the sale.

Here the loan with the highest priority (the first for $70,000) still gets paid with the first money. Then the loan with the next priority (the second for $20,000) is paid. However, there is only $5000 left after paying off the first; therefore, the second only gets $5000 despite the fact that the mortgage amount is for $20,000. Since there's no money left after this, the holder of the third receives nothing.

Case 3. The third mortgage forecloses; the first and second are current. The sale brings $10,000. Here the holder of the third mortgage gets the whole $10,000. The first and second mortgages, which were current, are unaffected. The successful buyer now has title to a piece of property with existing first and second mortgages on it. True, this buyer paid $10,000; however, there are already $90,000 of mortgages still on it.

Index

About the Author

Robert Irwin is one of America's foremost experts in every area of real estate. He is the author of McGraw-Hill's Tips & Traps series, as well as *The Home Buyer's Checklist, How to Get Started in Real Estate Investing,* and *How to Buy a Home When You Can't Afford It.*